THe
P🌸wer
OF A
P🙂sitive ™
friend 🤍

About the Authors

Best-selling author Karol Ladd offers lasting hope and biblical truth to women around the world through her Power of a Positive book series. A gifted communicator and dynamic leader, Karol is founder and president of Positive Life Principles, Inc., a resource company offering strategies for success in both home and business. Her vivacious personality makes her a popular speaker to women's organizations, church groups, and corporate events, and she is a frequent guest on radio and television programs. She is cofounder of USA Sonshine Girls, a character-building club for young girls, and serves on several educational boards. Her most valued role is that of wife to Curt and mother to daughters Grace and Joy. Visit her Web site at PositiveLifePrinciples.com.

Her best friend, Terry Ann Kelly, has an extensive background in public speaking: She has hosted local, regional, and nationally syndicated radio programs and has taught public speaking and business communication classes at Baylor, Dallas Baptist, and Belmont Universities. Inspiring audiences to impact their world for Christ, Terry Ann enjoys speaking to organizations and women's events on topics varying from home and family life to moral and social issues. She has appeared on programs such as *Politically Incorrect* and *Point of View* and writes articles for magazines and newspapers. Terry Ann finds her greatest fulfillment in meeting the needs of her husband and five school-age children.

THE P🌼WER OF A P☺sitive™ friend♡

Dr. Roby
Bad
doctor

HOWARD BOOKS
A DIVISION OF SIMON & SCHUSTER
New York   London   Toronto   Sydney

Karol Ladd and Terry Ann Kelly

Our purpose at Howard Books is to:

• *Increase faith* in the hearts of growing Christians

• *Inspire holiness* in the lives of believers

• *Instill hope* in the hearts of struggling people everywhere

Because He's coming again!

Published by Howard Books, a division of Simon & Schuster, Inc.
1230 Avenue of the Americas, New York, NY 10020
www.howardpublishing.com

The Power of a Positive Friend © 2004 by Karol Ladd and Terry Ann Kelly

Library of Congress Cataloging-in-Publication Data
Ladd, Karol.
     The power of a positive friend / Karol Ladd
          p. cm.
     Includes bibliographical references.
     ISBN 1-58229-344-9
     1. Christian women—Religious life. 2. Female friendship—Religious
aspects—Christianity. I. Title

     BV4527.L2512 2004
     241'.6762—dc22
                                                      2003056739

10 9 8 7 6 5 4

HOWARD is a registered trademark of Simon & Schuster, Inc.

Manufactured in the United States of America

For information regarding special discounts for bulk purchases, please contact Simon & Schuster Special Sales at 1-800-456-6798 or business@simonandschuster.com.

Some of the names used in the stories in this book are not the actual names; identifying details have been changed to protect anonymity. Any resemblance is purely coincidental.

Edited by Michele Buckingham
Interior design by Gabe Cardinale and John Luke
Cover design by LinDee Loveland

For our mothers,
Jo Ann Thompson and Barbara S. Kinder,
who showed us through their own godly example
the power of positive friendships.

Contents

Power Principle #4: The Power of Loyalty

Power Principle #5: The Power of Spiritual Bonds

Power Principle #6: The Power of Honesty

Power Principle #7: The Power of Forgiveness

Acknowledgments

A heart-filled thanks to Philis Boultinghouse, Michele Buckingham, Susan Wilson, and all our friends at Howard Publishing for the excellent work you did to make this book a blessing to others. And, finally, we want to thank our sisters (Karen, Tracy, and Julie) and our numerous friends who inspired many of the thoughts and stories in this book and encouraged us along the way. You are gifts from God to us.

*My purpose is that they may be encouraged in heart and united in love,
so that they may have the full riches of complete understanding, in order
that they may know the mystery of God, namely, Christ, in whom
are hidden all the treasures of wisdom and knowledge.*

—Colossians 2:2–3

Introduction

Treasures from Heaven
The Rich Value of a Positive Friend

Of all the things which wisdom provides to make life entirely happy, much the greatest is the possession of friendships.

—Epicurus

It's a miracle! After years of talking about writing a book together, we finally did it. There could be no better topic for us to write about than friendship. We have been the closest of friends since our freshman year in college. (We won't share with you how long ago that was.) As our friendship grew over the years, so did our list of ideas of "fun things to do together." Believe it or not, writing a book has always been at the top of the list.

The Power of a Positive Friend is about being a positive influence in the lives of other people. It is not a sweet and fluffy celebration of happy relationships. Rather, it is a compelling work designed to inspire and equip each and every one of us to build deeper and more meaningful friendships.

Writing this book caused us to take a serious look at the value of friendship in our own lives. We studied Scripture and examined principles that affect the potential for lasting relationships. In the process one thing became crystal clear: The worth of a good friend is priceless. Friendship is a topic that is deserving of our honor and attention.

The grim reality is that most people (including us!) juggle a myriad

1

of responsibilities and therefore struggle to make friendships a priority. Even as we began writing this book, we had difficulty finding a time slot on both of our overloaded calendars to get together for our initial brainstorming sessions. The mere fact that it was difficult to schedule a simple meeting drove home the point that the demands of life can easily chip away at the significant relationships in our lives. Developing and nurturing friendships in the fast lane of life is a veritable challenge!

But whether you are overly busy or lead a relatively simple life, the powerful principles for being a positive friend hold true. They are foundational and lasting, not because we decided they were important, but because they are based on God's Word. In the following pages, we show how these principles played out in the lives of Jonathan and David, Ruth and Naomi, Paul and Barnabas, and many other friends in the Bible. We look at Solomon's powerful advice on relationships in the Book of Proverbs. Most importantly, we observe Jesus' relationships with his disciples and followers as the perfect example of how to be a positive friend.

In addition, we share stories from history and from modern life to develop a rich and vibrant picture of the qualities that are evident in positive friendships. We also distribute meaningful quotes and Scripture verses throughout the pages. Our hope is that this book will enrich your current friendships and encourage you to pursue the potential of new and lasting ones. If you're married, we hope these relationship principles will even deepen your emotional connection with your spouse. After all, shouldn't husbands and wives be best friends?

A Reader-Friendly Plan

As you thumb through the pages, you will find that *The Power of a Positive Friend* is written in a reader-friendly format. The short chapters allow you to read a stimulating snippet here and there as time allows.

Take this book with you in your purse and read it while you are waiting in the carpool line or sitting in the doctor's office. Keep it on your bed stand and read a chapter or two before you turn out the light. The encouraging words and thought-provoking ideas will bring a smile to your face as you lay your head on your pillow for a good night's rest.

Of course, reading this book on your own will have powerful benefits, but you may also enjoy going over the chapters with a friend or group. Studying this book with other people can be a friendship builder in and of itself! The Power Point section at the end of each chapter offers a wonderful catalyst for discussion with others. Each Power Point provides a Scripture reading that applies to the topic in the chapter, along with questions to ask yourself or a group. It also suggests a sample prayer and a key verse to memorize.

Finally, the Power Point recommends an action step designed to help you put what you've learned from the chapter into practice. Reading a good book is fine; but when we take the time to practically apply its principles to our lives, it becomes all the more rich and valuable to us. We want this book to be more to you than a collection of nice words. We want it to be an encouragement to do as the apostle John says: "Let us not love with words or tongue but with actions and in truth" (1 John 3:18).

Pure Sonshine

Saint Thomas Aquinas said, "Friendship is the source of the greatest pleasures, and without friends even the most agreeable pursuits become tedious."[1] Positive friends are truly a pleasure. They add light and warmth to our lives. Negative friends, on the other hand, have a dark and chilling effect. When negative friends discourage us, gossip about us behind our backs, or continually argue with us, they drain and zap us of joy and strength.

My command is this: Love each other as I have loved you. —John 15:12

Understand, when we refer to positive friends, we're not talking about perky, happy-faced individuals who only tell us flattering platitudes. By positive friends we mean people who are a strengthening and uplifting influence in our lives. They build us up. They encourage us to do what is right and correct us when we get off base. We're better individuals because of them.

Perhaps you have never felt like a positive person. Maybe you're the "cup half empty" sort. Can you be a positive friend? Absolutely!

How? By allowing God's Holy Spirit to work in your life. He can and will develop positive qualities within you that will enrich all of your friendships. In Galatians 5:22–23 we read, "The fruit of the Spirit is love, joy, peace, patience, kindness, goodness, faithfulness, gentleness and self-control." Now those are positive qualities! And they are guaranteed to grow in our lives as we abide daily in Christ and allow the power of his Holy Spirit to flow through us.

It comes down to a choice. Will we allow God to work in us and through us to affect our relationships in a positive way? Or will we grovel and grope in self-centeredness, trying to interact with others in our own way, our own power, and our own strength? Ultimately, our love for others is a reflection of God's love toward us. The more we recognize and enjoy the fact that we are abundantly loved and forgiven by God, the easier it is for us to love and forgive others. As Jesus said, "Love each other as I have loved you" (John 15:12).

So join us now on a joyful journey! As you travel with us, believe that God's love through you can have a powerful and positive impact, not only on your friendships, but on your world. Be willing to shine brightly with his love—to allow it to pour through you to the people he places in your pathway. After all, our world is full of fractured and broken relationships. People all around us need to experience the power of a positive friend. Will that friend be you?

THE Gift OF A Positive friend

A friend is a present you give yourself.

—Robert Louis Stevenson

A mirror reflects a man's face, but what he is really like is shown by the kind of friends he chooses.

—Proverbs 27:19 TLB

A True Friend
The Blessing and Beauty of Kindred Spirits

A true friend is the greatest of all blessings.
—Francois de LaRochefoucauld

Have you ever felt lonely or in need of friends? Don't worry, you're not the only one. We've all been there.

It may have been a time when you moved to a different city, started a new job, or went to a new school, and every face you saw was unfamiliar. It may have been a time when you were surrounded by people but still felt alone, because you didn't have someone you could call a soul mate. Perhaps it was a time when something went wrong in your life and everyone you knew seemed to abandon you. As we began writing this book, we realized that almost all women, including ourselves, had felt that familiar tug of longing for an intimate friend.

Terry Ann reflects: A few short years ago, I sat on the old Chicago bricks that formed steps leading up to the front door of our home in Grapevine, Texas. It was a rare moment because my husband, Jay, who had just arrived home after being out of town for several days, was with me, and not one of our five children was in sight. Jay had picked up on the fact that I wasn't my usual not-a-care-in-the-world, goin'-and-blowin'

Friendship is a word the very sight of which in print makes the heart warm. —Augustine Birrell

self, and he wanted an explanation. I had ignored him and everyone else in our busy household all morning. One of the kids had asked, "What's wrong, Mom?" But of course I had replied (like any other woman), "Oh, nothing. I just don't have anything to say."

Now, believe me when I say that for me to be quiet, disconnected, placid, and nonexpressive, I have to be either extremely ill, deeply offended, or highly depressed, and I don't mean clinically. But you know how we women are. We really do want to let our family members know that something is wrong, but we want them to drag it out of us. We want to pout for a significant amount of time, while they plead for us to tell them why we are so blue.

So Jay began, "I know something is wrong. Don't you want to talk about it?" He was going to leave for the baseball fields with the boys in a few minutes, so I knew this was my last chance to get what I wanted: sympathy.

"I don't have any friends!" I blurted out.

It was all Jay could do not to laugh out loud. But he held it in and did what any good husband would do. He gave me about three minutes to tell him what was on my heart. But he refused to come to my "pity party," declaring, "You have more friends than anybody I know. You never meet a stranger."

So much for nurturing. *Why was I feeling this way? Why was I feeling overwhelmed and depressed? Why was I feeling friendless?*

Thinking back, it's no wonder I was discouraged that morning. Just look at the schedule I kept the day before I decided that "nobody loves me, everybody hates me, I think I'll go eat worms!"

6:00 A.M. Rise and shine; get five children ready for the day.

7:30 A.M. Drive oldest four to school.

9:30 A.M. Drive youngest child to "mother's day out."

9:45 A.M. Attempt to be on time for my doctor's appointment.

11:30 A.M. Pick up oldest child, Katelin, from school to home-school half a day.

12:00 P.M. Start Katelin on homework and remind her to walk to piano at 2:00.

1:00 P.M. Arrive at doctor's office for second appointment.

2:30 P.M. Pick up youngest child from school.

2:45 P.M. Pick up Katelin from piano.

2:55 P.M. Pick up other three from school.

3:20 P.M. Take Colt to piano.

3:30 P.M. Take Katelin to voice lesson.

3:35 P.M. Take Clay to orthodontist appointment.

4:00 P.M. Pick up Colt from piano.

4:15 P.M. Pick up Katelin from voice lesson.

4:30 P.M. Pick up Clay from orthodontist.

It was at this point, in the orthodontist's parking lot, that I had a quick cry. I would have cried longer, but I didn't have time. Two of my sons had to get home to get dressed for baseball practice at two different fields; another son had a baseball game; and Katelin, if my memory serves me right, had basketball practice.

That evening, when everyone was finally home, I oversaw home-work, baths, and goodnight prayers. I think we must have eaten dinner at some point. I also did the laundry, cleaned the dishes, signed school papers, fed two dogs, and took them outside—all the while knowing that Jay, whose job requires him to travel, was relaxing in a hotel some-where, flipping the television stations with a remote control.

I could blame my busyness on having five children. But I feel confident that no matter what our life circumstances might be, most of us are still busy with *something*. Whether you are a single woman with a full-time job, a grandmother raising your grandchildren, a mom who works away from home or in the home full time, it's all the same: We're busy!

So when my husband tried to console me on the front porch of our home, listening to me sob that I didn't have any friends, what he should have discerned was that I needed time with one of my "bosom buddies." Because in actuality, what was wrong was not that I didn't have any friends; it was that I hadn't spent any meaningful, heart-to-heart time with any of those friends in *forever*.

❀ ❀ ❀

The Longing for Intimate Friendships

Deep and abiding friendships are keenly important to women. That's the way we're made. In her book *A Woman's Search for Worth*, Dr. Deborah Newman points to the creation of the first woman as the key to understanding our desire for relationships: "The creation of man and woman were unique from each other. After the man was created, he opened his eyes, and the first thing he saw was God; the second thing he saw was the garden. When the woman was created, she opened her eyes, and the first thing she saw was God; the second thing she saw was Adam."[1]

Dr. Newman goes on to say that the first woman was created in the context of relationships—as man's helpmate. That first woman, Eve, was also cursed in the area of relationships, as we read in Genesis 3:16 after that fateful bite of forbidden fruit: "To the woman [God] said, 'I will greatly increase your pains in childbearing; with pain you will give birth to children. Your desire will be for your husband, and he will rule over you.'"

From the very beginning, women have needed relationships. And from the beginning, we've struggled with them.

Deep within every woman's heart is the desire to connect with another individual. The problem is, we live in such a fast-paced society that we rarely have time to develop and maintain meaningful relationships with others. "Let's do lunch" and "Call me sometime" are phrases we often say but seldom do. Society places great pressure on us to be the best, look the best, feel the best, work the best, decorate the best, buy the best, mother the best, and wife the best. Then, after we've worked on being the best we can be, we feel compelled to ensure that our children or grandchildren are given the best opportunities for success in school and on the playing field. We just *have* to get them to soccer, football, baseball, basketball, and cheerleading practices. Did we mention piano, voice, dance, and drama lessons? And really, we should squeeze in church activities too.

Whew! After all that, who has time for a relaxing cup of coffee over the back fence with a neighbor? We may not even know some of our neighbors' first names! Yet many of us are lonely for the kind of relationship Aunt Bee had with Clara on *The Andy Griffith Show.* Our husbands may be wonderful, but they can't play the part of Aunt Bee. We long to visit the slow-paced town of Mayberry, where Clara and Bee lived. But most of us live in a place called Hurryville, where we have:

- One-hour photo processing
- Ten-minute lube jobs
- One-day dry cleaners
- Fast-food lunches
- Disposable plates and plastic silverware (Who has time to do dishes?)
- Microwave ovens

True, positive friendship can't be cooked in a microwave! It must be crock-pot simmered over time. The quality ingredients of friendship need this type of slow cooking to gradually blend and melt together. The result is the soul-nurturing food of a truly meaningful relationship.

The Birth of a Friendship

Our own friendship has been simmering for twenty-five years. It began in the fall of 1978 when we were freshmen at Baylor University in Waco, Texas. We met in Collins Dorm; Terry Ann lived on the sixth floor and Karol on the fourth. As we got to know each other, we just seemed to click. But it wasn't till we met at Crystal's Pizza Palace during spring break of our freshman year that we recognized the potential for a lifelong friendship.

As we talked over pizza, we began to realize that we had quite a few life experiences in common. Both of our dads were in the insurance business, and both of our moms were sweet, selfless, godly women. We both came from all-girl families (with the exceptions of our lucky dads). Our spiritual journeys were also very similar; we both became Christians and dedicated our lives to serving Christ at an early age.

A new friendship was born that day at Crystal's Pizza Palace in Irving, Texas. Kindred spirits had been discovered! We both drove away from that lunch with a warm place in our hearts, knowing that we had the potential of becoming lasting friends. In our sophomore year, we became suite mates in Alexander Dorm; and from that point on, our "friendship of the heart" was cemented.

❦

Terry Ann reflects: Karol taught me how to be more relaxed while, oddly enough, still leading an extremely disciplined life. I remember the year Karol trained for a marathon and never seemed to miss a workout or forget to eat her "carbs." And I'll never forget the morning I woke up early and couldn't find my roomie in the apartment. I looked everywhere for her and began to get a little worried. Finally I swung open her closet door and there she was, on her knees, with her face buried in her hands. She was in prayer. To this day that is my fondest and most impacting memory of Karol. She truly exemplified the disciplines of the Christian life that have been the backbone of my most significant friendship.

Karol reflects: At Baylor, everyone knew Terry Ann. She was the freshman homecoming queen, class representative, and all-around Miss Personality. A true sanguine! She taught me things like the importance of wearing lipstick, how to use a sun lamp to the point of having your eyes swell shut, and how to create the "big hair" look we Texas women are famous for.

I was always amazed at the way Terry Ann could walk into a class and take a test without really studying. Whenever I asked her how she did it, she always replied, "Oh, it's just common sense!" Terry Ann was blessed with a great deal of common sense and wisdom. She was the epitome of a woman who feared the Lord and followed his will—even down to which boy she asked to a sorority function.

One particular time will live in my memory forever. Terry Ann wanted to ask a young man named Mark—the heartthrob of practically every girl on campus—to the Pi Phi dance, but she just wasn't sure if she should. She was always careful about dating and about hearing God in such matters. So she asked me to kneel and pray with her. "If I'm supposed to ask Mark to go to the dance with me," she implored the Lord, "then have Mark call me and ask me out first."

Now, mind you, Mark and Terry Ann barely knew each other at the time she prayed this prayer. I must admit my faith was weak. But not Terry Ann's. She was firm in her resolve to submit this matter to God.

Love one another deeply, from the heart. —1 Peter 1:22

13

Brrrrring! The phone rang not five minutes after we finished praying. Guess who it was? You got it! Mark called and asked Terry Ann on a date. Oh me of little faith! In the years that followed I continued to marvel at the complete faith Terry Ann had in God and her total willingness to submit to his work in her life. Her faith is a testimony to me to this day.

❁ ❁ ❁

What Kind of Friend Am I?

When we were brainstorming ideas for this book, we began to see even more clearly how significant our relationship was and is to us. We recognized that our hurried lifestyles often foster surface friendships but leave little room for nurturing deep and quality ones. In a culture characterized by hyper-speed lifestyles and cyber connections, true, deep, and positive friendships are a rare commodity.

What is the solution? Is it to slow down our lives and make better use of our time? If the key to having lasting, more meaningful relationships were as simple as better time management, then we could all read a book on how to organize our time—and *voila!* We would increase our number of friends. Yet we all know women who are highly organized but still wallow in the depths of loneliness. Equally, we know women with packed schedules who seem to have thriving relationships. Although we should always reexamine our overbusy schedules and cut out what isn't necessary, slowing down is not necessarily the answer.

For some women, being too busy has never been an issue. Their struggle is with a lack of self-confidence or the fear of getting too close to others. Some have hurtful issues from the past that affect their present relationships. Others long to have quality relationships, but they're not quite sure how to go about it.

So what is the key to connecting? Perhaps your parents, like ours, taught you when you were quite young that to have a friend, you must be a friend. How true. But what does it mean to be a friend? What does a friend look like? And how would you describe yourself in the context of relationships?

Before you read any further, grab a pen, get a cup of hot tea, curl up in a comfy chair, and take a few moments to thoughtfully complete the following friendship self-assessment. (Go ahead—get your pen and tea. We'll wait right here until you get back.) As you fill out this assessment, you will begin to ponder two important questions: "Am I a friend to others?" and "What type of friendships do I have in my life?" Don't worry; there are no right or wrong answers. The inventory is meant to be introspective. Just answer honestly, based on your own experience and perspective on friendship.

The Friendship Self-Assessment Inventory

1. My personal definition of friendship is:_____

   _____

   _____

   _____

   _____

   _____

   _____

2. Based on my personal definition of friendship, I currently have (circle one)…

   three or fewer friends.

   four to ten friends.

   eleven to twenty-five friends.

   twenty-six to fifty friends.

fifty-one to one hundred friends.

more than one hundred friends.

3. Developing friendships…

    is easy for me.

    is something I have to work at.

    is difficult for me.

4. What is it about this time in my life that makes it difficult for me to find time for friends?_____

_____

_____

5. Today I feel…

    that I have meaningful, quality friendships.

    that I would like to have more significant friendships.

    that I need to learn how to be a better friend.

    that a strong relationship with God and my family is all I
      need.

6. Characteristics I long for in a friendship are: _____

_____

_____

7. The way I demonstrate positive friendship to others is:_____

_____

_____

There, now, that wasn't so difficult—was it? Our hope is that this assessment drew out thoughts and feelings about friendship that you've had stored up inside. Hopefully it provoked you to think about your personal understanding of relationships in a fresh, new way. After all, most of us have never taken a course on positive friendship. We've simply learned about relating to others from the School of Hard Knocks and our own life experiences.

As we journey through the rest of this book together, we will explore the positive qualities that make each of us better friends. In the process we hope that you, along with us, will begin to enrich the friendships you already have, even as you discover ways to develop new ones. Our prayer is that before the last page is turned, we will have learned together to be positive friends who bring mutual blessing into each other's lives.

POWER POINT

● **Read:** Genesis chapters 2 and 3. What is it about the creation of woman that makes her unique? Name some relational qualities that you see mostly in women.

♡ **Pray:** Wonderful and loving heavenly Father, thank you for the way you created me as a woman. Thank you for the friendships you have placed in my life. Bless my relationships and help me to see my role as a friend more clearly. Allow me to develop the qualities of a good and positive friend. You alone offer the example of a true and perfect friend. Let your Holy Spirit love and live through me. In Jesus' name I pray, amen.

♀ **Remember:** "Dear friends, let us love one another, for love comes from God. Everyone who loves has been born of God and knows God" (1 John 4:7).

☺ **Do:** Take a moment to think about one of your dearest friends and what she has meant to you in your life. Write out a fond memory you have of her, and send it to her along with a card. You will bring a smile to two faces—yours and hers!

The Spice of Life
Recognizing the Variety of Friendships
God Puts in Your Life

Blessed are they who have the gift of making friends, for it is one of God's best gifts. It involves many things, but above all, the power of getting out of one's self and appreciating whatever is noble and loving in another.

—Thomas Hughes

The word *friend* is much like the word *love*. We use it to mean many different things. When we say we love God, for example, we are giving a different meaning to the word *love* than when we say we love French fries. So what do we really mean when we call someone a "friend"?

Perhaps you found yourself wondering that very thing as you worked your way through the Friendship Self-Assessment Inventory in chapter 1. Many people will flow in and out of our lives, and most will never become true and abiding friends—the kind we connect with, heart-to-heart. So who are all these people we interact with daily, and what factors determine whether or not they become our friends?

The Influence of Personality

All of us know someone who never seems to meet a stranger. She's the woman who can be passing through the state of Idaho on vacation, and when she stops at a gas station in the middle of nowhere to fill up her minivan, she recognizes the station attendant as someone she went to high school with in Kentucky thirty years before. This woman appears to have an endless number of friends! On the other hand, we all know someone else who is the total opposite; she's the woman who seems quite content to have relationships with only a handful of friends. What accounts for the difference?

A big part of the answer is found in the fact that God has given each of us a wonderful and unique personality. Our personalities, or temperaments, influence the way we make friends. Tim LaHaye, in his 1973 classic, *The Spirit-Controlled Temperament,* identifies four basic personality types that more or less describe most of us. Here is a brief synopsis of the qualities of each one.

1. *Choleric:* Strong-willed, determined, independent, optimistic, practical, productive, decisive, confident, a leader. Weaknesses include: angry, cruel, sarcastic, domineering, inconsiderate, proud, unemotional.

2. *Sanguine:* Talkative, outgoing, enthusiastic, warm, personable, friendly, compassionate, carefree. Weaknesses include: weak-willed, unstable, undisciplined, restless, undependable, egocentric, loud, tendency to exaggerate.

3. *Melancholy:* Gifted, analytical, sensitive, a perfectionist, aesthetic, idealistic, loyal, self-sacrificing. Weaknesses include: self-centered, moody, negative, unsociable, critical, revengeful, rigid.

4. *Phlegmatic:* Calm, easy-going, dependable, efficient, conservative, practical, diplomatic, humorous. Weaknesses include: stingy, fearful, indecisive, a spectator, self-protective, selfish, unmotivated.[1]

Do you see yourself in one of these descriptions? Can you see how the number of friends you have may be influenced by your God-given temperament? A sanguine woman, for example, may have hundreds of friends, but many of those friendships are likely to be surface-level. A melancholy woman, on the other hand, may have only a handful of friends, but those relationships are probably tried and true.

❀

Terry Ann reflects: Karol says I am the typical sanguine. Not long ago, I was working out at a gym and noticed a man next to me pumping iron. I felt confident that I knew him from somewhere. You've heard it said, "Curiosity kills the cat"—well, I couldn't stand not knowing why he seemed so familiar.

Inside my head I could hear my husband saying, "Terry Ann, don't walk up to a stranger, especially a man, and say, 'Don't I know you from somewhere?' That is the oldest pick-up line in history." But I knew my motives were pure. Besides, I was sure I'd gone to school with him at some point. Or maybe we shopped at the same grocery store back in 1984.

I worked out a little longer, all the while hoping we would make eye contact so I could say something to him. Finally I took the plunge. I knew my husband wouldn't approve, but my overzealous, never-met-a-stranger nature took over.

"I know this sounds like a pick-up line," I started, "but trust me, it's not, because I have five children—and by the way, two of them are downstairs in the kids play area—and I'm happily married, and I really shouldn't be saying this, but—don't I know you from somewhere?"

He stared at me blankly. After I finally quit talking and came up for air, he said, "No, I'm just visiting. I'm from Arkansas." Oh well!

Often times when I strike up a conversation with strangers in the presence of my husband, he'll nudge me and say, "Terry Ann, be quiet. They don't care." You see, he has a different personality type, and he is quite content with the relationships he currently has. He sees no pressing need to initiate relationships with new people, since he feels he's too busy to spend much time with the friends he already cares about!

❧ ❧ ❧

Extrovert or Introvert?

Another aspect of personality that influences our friendships is whether we are extroverted or introverted. Corporate America uses a testing instrument called the Myers Briggs Type Indicator to measure, among other things, people's tendencies towards extroversion or introversion. Participants are asked to answer a number of test questions based on their preferences in different life situations. The interesting thing about this measure is that the extroversion/introversion scale is not based on whether a person is outgoing or shy. Rather, it's based on how a person gets his or her energy "recharged." Does the person get charged up by being with other people? Or does he or she find renewal in solitude and inner contemplation?

Take Ethel Extrovert, for instance. She seems to know everybody in town—or in the state for that matter. She loves to be around other people. She finds their lives interesting and stimulating. She is forever asking them about their families, their work, and other life circumstances. When she goes to a party, she comes home invigorated.

Irene Introvert, on the other hand, would attend the same party and come home exhausted, maybe overwhelmed. Small talk for Irene is laborious. For that matter, she's not comfortable in most social situations that involve a large number of people. In order to get her life battery revved up, Irene much prefers to be left alone with a good book or a quiet CD. Solitude is what gets her up and going and ready to take on the day.

We can never replace a friend. When a man is fortunate enough to have several, he finds they are all different. No one has a double in friendship. —Friedrich von Schiller

22

Over their lifetimes, Ethel will know and purposefully interact with hundreds and possibly thousands more people than Irene will. And that's okay! It's just the way God made each of them.

In Psalm 139:13–14, God's Word tells us, "For you created my inmost being; you knit me together in my mother's womb. I praise you because I am fearfully and wonderfully made; your works are wonderful, I know that full well." We need to be confident that God created us, personality and all, just the way he wants us to be. So often we envy the woman who appears to have personality plus. Instead, we need to recognize and honor the fact that God created us in such a way that we are fully equipped to do the work he has planned for us. He foreknew from the beginning of time the number of people he would bring into our lives. He knew exactly which ones he wanted us to bless and which ones he wanted us to learn from.

The fact that God has uniquely equipped us for our task doesn't mean we should be satisfied to stay on the far ends of the extrovert/introvert scale, however. We should all strive for balance. The Irene Introverts of the world, after spending quality time alone in prayer, really need to force themselves to look for opportunities to be with people in order to share their lives with others. They shouldn't assume, "I'm most comfortable in my solitude. Therefore it must not be my job to reach out to others."

The Ethel Extroverts, meanwhile, need to force themselves to be alone and quiet with God before they go out to be with others. Ethels shouldn't allow their natural inclination of relating and communicating to lead to idle, useless chatter and unnecessary relationships. Extroverts like Ethel can end up wasting their time with people God never intended for them to reach or minister to. They must learn to seek God in solitude and trust him to guide their relationships.

The Circles of Friendship

As we've said, the number of friends we have depends a great deal upon our God-given personalities. But what *kinds* of friends are we talking about? Going back to our question at the beginning of this chapter: What do we really mean when we call someone a "friend"?

The following diagram of concentric circles helps us define the significance of the relationships we have in our lives. As you can see, there are three basic levels of friendship:

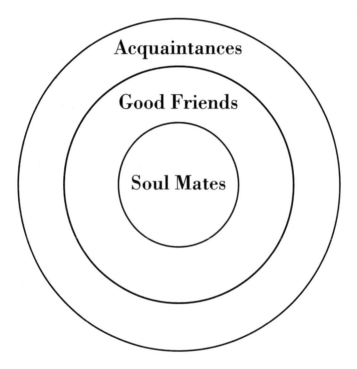

In our lifetimes we will have a much larger circle of acquaintances than good friends. Our circle of good friends will be larger than our circle of soul mates. Why is this? Let's take a few moments to look at the characteristics of each group.

Acquaintances

The outer circle represents the large group of acquaintances we come into contact with in life. These are the people we know, but not intimately or well—the woman who always sits behind us in church, the neighbor down the street, the clerk at the dry cleaner's. Typically, an acquaintance is someone we interact with on no more than a surface level. We don't choose our acquaintances; they just happen, based on where our day-to-day living takes us.

For extreme introverts, the circle of acquaintances may include as few as twenty people. For extreme extroverts, the circle may include literally thousands. The important thing to remember is that the number of acquaintances a woman has doesn't determine if she is a good or bad friend. It simply reflects her personality type.

It also reflects a second factor: her level of involvement in activities outside the home. For example, does she work in an office? Go to school? Take her kids to school? How involved is she in her church and her community?

❁

Karol reflects: In a typical year, Terry Ann has many more opportunities to make acquaintances than I do. The main reason is that she has five children, and I have two. The law of multiplicity simply goes into effect.

Each year, because of her children's activities, Terry Ann meets an average of fourteen or fifteen recreational team coaches, fifteen to twenty-five school teachers, and five to ten Sunday school teachers. I, on the other hand, get to know five or six coaches, ten to twelve school teachers, and two to four Sunday school teachers.

❁ ❁ ❁

The fact is, some of us are involved in more activities outside the home than others. And the more involved we are, quite naturally, the more acquaintances we have. But do these acquaintance-level friendships really matter? They do, if we believe that people matter to God!

The Lord Jesus had many acquaintances. He recognized the value of every person he met. He understood that his job was to point the way to the Father to every person whose life touched his, however briefly. That was his mission, his passion, his calling. Remember, Jesus was not only God in human form; he was also completely man. He had parents, brothers, and sisters. He had a job. Carpentry was his trade until he entered full-time public ministry at the age of thirty. He went to weddings, funerals, and the market. He led a human life that caused him to naturally interact with others every day.

In the process he had relationships with people he didn't necessarily choose to spend close, intimate time with. He had unscheduled interaction with people day in and day out. One of these was Zacchaeus, the "wee little man," as the children's song says, who desired to catch a glimpse of the famous teacher. Zacchaeus did not hold the same values as Jesus. As a matter of fact, we read in Luke 19:7 that the crowd murmured when they saw that Jesus was going to be the houseguest of a sinner. Jesus, however, took that encounter with Zacchaeus as an opportunity to point him to the Truth.

Did Zacchaeus ever become more than an acquaintance to Jesus? We can't be sure. But this we know: People counted to Jesus—all people. He looked at "chance" meetings with individuals as divine appointments for drawing them to the Father.

Are we like Jesus with the acquaintances God brings across our paths? Are we sensitive to God's Spirit within us, so that we recognize opportunities to minister God's truth—say, to the lady we meet in the grocery store line or the teller at the bank? Our acquaintances should matter to us, because they matter to God!

Good Friends

Good friends are drawn from our circle of acquaintances. Who is a good friend? Imagine for a moment that you are surprising your husband with a birthday party. Who would you invite? You are giving your parents a fortieth anniversary celebration. Who would come? You decide to have a Christmas luncheon and ornament exchange in your home. Who would make the guest list? These "chosen" people are your good friends.

Another word for "good friend" is *companion*. A companion, by definition, is a person who associates with or accompanies another. Who are the people who are willing to accompany us in life? They're usually the ones who are like-minded on issues that matter. They're the ones who have something in common with us that causes our paths to cross on a regular basis in day-to-day living. Companions are distinct from acquaintances in that we've made a "beyond the surface" connection with them. They are kindred spirits of sorts.

Perhaps you, like us, have found that many of your good friendships have developed from among fellow mothers who have children the same ages as your own. You've shared splintery bleachers at the baseball field or swapped babysitting duties so you both could get to your dreaded annual OB/GYN appointments. Or perhaps your friendships have developed from among coworkers as you've worked on projects together, discovering common interests in the process. One way or another, life circumstances have provided opportunities for you to be together consistently enough to discover a heart connection.

Jesus himself had many companions. We think first of the twelve disciples, but there were others as well—people like Lazarus, Mary, and Martha; John the Baptist; and Nicodemus. Interestingly enough, before he selected his disciples, Jesus prayed to God for guidance. He knew that good friends must be chosen carefully. Not all acquaintances are "good friend" material! As George Washington said, "Associate yourself with men of good quality if you esteem your own reputation, for 'tis better to be alone than in bad company."[2] If the Son of God saw the need to seek his Father's counsel regarding friendships, how much more do we, in all our human frailty, need guidance in choosing good friends?

Proverbs 12:26 reminds us, "A righteous man is cautious in friendship, but the way of the wicked leads them astray." The plain truth is that we become like the people we hang around with. Paul was well aware of the powerful effect friends can have on each other. He warned the early Christians to avoid becoming too close with people who were not walking with Christ: "But now I am writing you that you must not associate with anyone who calls himself a brother but is sexually immoral or greedy, an idolater or a slanderer, a drunkard or a swindler. With such a man [friend] do not even eat" (1 Corinthians 5:11).

Paul's point is clear. We are not to choose as good friends people who are unwise or involved in corrupt lifestyles. This doesn't mean we have the right to sit in judgment over others; it simply means we must use discernment in our choice of companions. Certainly we should love all people, as Christ did. But also like Christ, we must use discernment in deciding with whom we will walk hand in hand.

Many of us have no problem warning our teenagers about the ever-lurking danger of so-called "friends" who might lead them down the wrong path. But what about our own companions? Are they a positive influence in our lives? We need to look at the women we surround ourselves with and ask:

- Do they encourage us to make wise choices?

- Do they help us to elevate our thinking? For example, do they help us take our focus off material things and encourage us to be satisfied with the incredible gifts God has blessed us with?

- Do they rejoice in our success, mourn in our grief, motivate in our laziness, confront in our sin, comfort in our illness, laugh in our joy?

If we can answer yes to these questions, then we are truly blessed! Volney Streamer put it this way, "We inherit our relatives and our features and may not escape them; but we can select our clothing and our friends, and let us be careful that both fit us."[3]

Selecting and then nurturing a good friendship requires effort. How much effort? That depends. Some women seem to have a natural ability to make friends. Others have to study and practice the art of friendship with a vengeance in order to develop just a few of their acquaintances into valued companions. Fortunately, when it comes to friends, each day is a new beginning. It doesn't matter where we are in our friendship pilgrimage; when the sun comes up each morning, our quest for more meaningful relationships begins anew.

As the ancient Roman poet Horace said, *"Carpe diem!"*—Seize the day! We need to program our minds and hearts to see the minutes and hours that fill each day as opportunities to bless others with our friendship. Who knows? Today may be the day we have the privilege of giving away hope or laughter to someone who is in despair. It may be the day we have the chance to encourage someone who is hurting with an uplifting phone call or poignant card. It may be the day we open the eyes of our hearts and discover that an acquaintance has become a good friend.

These things won't just "happen" unless we view life as purposeful—unless we believe that God allows people and circumstances into our lives on purpose in order to form us into someone who looks and acts more like Jesus. Even now he has someone waiting around the corner—or standing behind us in line or browsing the shelves at the video store—who has the potential to become our new good friend.

Soul Mates

Jesus said in John 15:13, "Greater love has no one than this, that he lay down his life for his friends." Wow! That's a sobering statement. Think for a moment: Is there anyone you call "friend" who would do that for you? Is there someone (other than a person in your immediate family) for whom you would put *your* life on the line? That person is more than a good friend. He or she is a true friend of the heart—a soul mate.

Perhaps it's difficult for you to think about laying down your life in a physical sense for someone else. Even in light of the new threat of terrorism, God, in his grace, has afforded those of us in America a relatively safe and secure environment in which to experience life. So here's another way to ask the question: Is there someone with whom you are willing to risk revealing your every thought, emotion, fault, desire, and ambition? Someone for whom you always lay out the welcome mat at the door of your heart?

If so, you have found that deepest level of human communion. Friendships of the heart are rare and valuable. But they are something all of us can possess if we're willing to pay the price. After all, anything worth having is costly. The price we pay for a friend that, as Proverbs 18:24 says, "sticks closer than a brother," is high. It's called *vulnerability.*

We may share opinions and beliefs with a companion, but we share our hearts with a soul mate. Opening our lives to another person to that degree can be frightening. We take a risk when we lay out the welcome mat to our hearts. Will it be well worn over time, or will it be

30

trampled upon? The risk is worth taking, however, because a soul mate makes our lives rich in ways no one else can.

Jesus knew this. Scripture indicates that while Jesus had large numbers of acquaintances and many good friends, he shared his heart on a more intimate level with three men in particular: Peter, James, and John. These soul mates were repeatedly singled out to participate in the most significant events of Jesus' life on earth, including the transfiguration (Matthew 17:1–13) and Jesus' final hours in the Garden of Gethsemane (Matthew 26:36–46).

Like Jesus, we all want to have soul mates who will be with us to share in our times of darkest struggle as well as our moments of brightest joy. But true soul mates are few and far between. Count yourself lucky if you have two or three of these most prized of relationships in your entire lifetime! (Of course, if you're married, your husband should fall into this category. Sadly, many husbands and wives live day-in and day-out at little more than the acquaintance level. If your spouse has drifted away—or you've pushed him—from the inner circle of your life, use the principles of positive friendship to draw him back in.)

Soul-mate friendships don't happen overnight. Just as it takes time for good friends to emerge from the acquaintance circle, it may take years for a soul mate to develop from the companionship level. Not every good friend will become a soul mate, but a precious few will. The goal is not to collect the largest number of friends; it's to have the most meaningful relationships possible.

Friendship Defined

Many years ago an English publication offered a prize for the best definition of a friend. Here are a few of the responses among the thousands that were received. A friend is:

There are different kinds of gifts, but the same Spirit. There are different kinds of service, but the same Lord. There are different kinds of working, but the same God works all of them in all men. —1 Corinthians 12:4–6

31

- "One who multiplies joys and divides grief"

- "One who understands our silence"

- "A volume of sympathy bound in cloth"

- "A watch that beats true for all time and never runs down"

Here's the definition that won the prize:

- "A friend is the one who comes in when the whole world has gone out"[4]

All of us need friends who will "come in when the whole world has gone out." And all of us should strive to be that kind of friend to others. Let's appreciate and nurture the variety of friendships that God brings into our lives. As we do, we'll discover the great power that is found in having—and being—a positive friend.

POWER POINT

⚙ **Read:** Psalm 139. As you read these verses, rejoice in the fact that God has made you special and unique. What qualities has God uniquely given you that will enable you to be a positive friend?

▷ **Pray:** Dear and wonderful Lord, there is no better soul mate than you! I'm so glad that you desire to be much more than an acquaintance in my life. I desire to draw close to you. As I fellowship with you, please develop the wonderful qualities of your Spirit within my life, and use my unique personality, gifts, and talents to make a difference in the lives of others. Help me discover the kindred spirits around me, and open my eyes to those who are potential soul mates. May I appreciate each relationship you bring into my life. Help me to nurture and develop only the friendships you desire for me to have. In Jesus' name I pray, amen.

💡 **Remember:** "I praise you because I am fearfully and wonderfully made; your works are wonderful, I know that full well" (Psalm 139:14).

☺ **Do:** On a blank sheet of paper, draw a larger version of the three concentric circles of friendship illustrated in this chapter. In the acquaintance circle, jot down the names of people who come to mind. Don't belabor this; you won't be able to name everyone you know! Then fill in the good friend circle and soul mate circle with the names of current friends in your life. Is there someone in the good friend category who may have the potential of becoming a soul mate? Watch and pray for opportunities to grow closer to this person. Consider giving her a quick call to say hello or invite her to lunch.

Power Principle #1

THe P✿wer OF s☺ster☺☺d

*Let love for your fellow believers continue and be a fixed
practice with you [never let it fail].*

—Hebrews 13:1 AMP

It is that my friends have made the story of my life. In a thousand ways they have turned my limitations into beautiful privileges, and enabled me to walk serene and happy in the shadow cast by my deprivation.

—Helen Keller

The Tie That Bonds Hearts
Building on Your Common Interests

Some friendships are made by nature; some by contract,
some by interest, and some by souls.

—Jeremy Taylor

The sound of breaking glass was almost deafening as the three test tubes fell from the table and were dashed into thousands of pieces on the hard tile floor. After that you could have heard a pin drop. The forty-two eyes of twenty-one students and the glaring stare of the teacher went directly to Marianne.

A freshman in a new high school, Marianne struggled with her self-image. It was hard enough going through adolescence; being the awkward "new girl" made life even harder. Only six weeks into school, and Marianne had already earned the reputation of being clumsy and uncoordinated. Just last week she had poured the wrong chemical into the beaker and had botched the science experiment for her group. The week before, she had tripped coming into the classroom and landed in a heap in front of the instructor's desk. And now this! Three broken test tubes and a roomful of accusing stares were too much for a friendless fourteen-year-old to bear.

Suddenly the girl standing next to her blurted out, "Oh, I'm sorry, Mrs. Thompson. I didn't mean to knock them over. It was so clumsy of me."

Marianne looked on in disbelief as Hailey, one of her lab partners, quickly took the blame for her mistake. As Mrs. Thompson hurried to help clean up the mess and the rest of the students went back to their work, all Marianne could manage was a grateful whisper of "Thank you."

"Don't worry about it. No big deal" was the hushed reply.

For six weeks Hailey had watched in anguish as Marianne continued to embarrass herself with her self-conscious awkwardness. Hailey knew the pain that Marianne felt, because she, too, had been the "new girl" almost more times than she could count. She had even moved three times during one school year! Hailey knew the feeling of wanting to fit in so bad that you try too hard.

As the class ended and the bell rang, the girls walked into the hallway together possessing something far more valuable than three glass test tubes. They had a common bond. They'd discovered the seeds of a budding friendship that would eventually grow into a strong, positive force in their lives, helping them both get through the difficult high-school years.

All friendships of the heart have something in common—a thread that first knits the two hearts together. Make a mental note right now of your most significant friendship. What was it that first drew the two of you to one another? Was it a common hobby or an interest in the same type of music? Was it similar life circumstances—for example, husbands who work for the same company or children who attend the same day care? Did you serve on a civic, school, or church committee together? Maybe you met in a grocery-store line and simply shared how you were surviving the joys of motherhood. Or maybe a co-worker in the office became a co-laborer in life as your friendship grew strong outside the workplace.

We need to keep our eyes open to recognize the common threads that connect us to other women. Maybe you relate all too well to Marianne and Hailey. You continually put down roots, only to have your life jerked out of the ground and thrust into a new environment time and time again. You'd like to have a friend, but you're not sure you want to put your heart on the line once more. Your eyes are closed, mostly for self-protection.

Or maybe you have lived in the same community for years. You don't feel the need to make a new friend; you're comfortable with life the way it is. You may have things in common with other people, but you don't notice because you're not interested in potential new friendships.

At times all of us find ourselves in a friendship rut. The busyness of our lives, our habitual routines, and our past experiences can cause us to be blinded to new, life-giving relationships that the Lord has for us.

Birth of a Sisterhood

Have you ever had an "aha moment"—that instant of realization that you have a connection, a common interest, or a bond with someone? Let's say you run into an acquaintance—someone you know, but not well. You start out talking on a typically surface level. "Hello, how are you?" "Fine, how are you?" "Nice day isn't it?" Then something changes—some small turn in the conversation reveals a morsel of potential for a deeper connection or understanding, and a budding friendship is born.

❖

Karol reflects: The cold bleachers at my daughter's soccer game provided the setting for an aha moment for me. Sally, Reeve, and I sat bundled up, watching our kindergarten daughters play soccer. The season had just started, so we barely knew each other. But somewhere between "Go Sarah!" and "Kick the ball, *kick the ball!*" we had an aha moment.

It began with a simple question. Sally asked me, "Are you signing up your daughter for Scouts?" Oddly, I had just finished reading an article in a Christian magazine that expressed some concerns about the scouting organization. Sally had read the same article. Our eyes brightened as we shared a connection and a mutual understanding. Reeve joined the conversation and shared similar concerns.

As the three of us watched our girls running on the field, we talked about what we could do as an alternative to the scout program. By the end of the game, we were well on our way to putting together a whole new program for kids at our daughters' school. And by the time the soccer season rounded to a close, we had become fast friends in the planning process.

The next school year we were ready to launch our new program together. We called it "Sonshine Girls." We worked through the many first-year kinks, prayed through multiple challenges, and drew close together in deep friendship. Sonshine Girls still meets today (nine years later), and numerous clubs have popped up throughout the community. On those freezing soccer fields a new organization was started—but more importantly, a sisterhood between Reeve, Sally, and me was born.

❖ ❖ ❖

Aha moments happen all around us. Our job is to recognize them as relationship opportunities and build on them. Look for aha moments when you volunteer for a service group or ministry. Be aware of them when you attend a Bible study. Recognize them as you take a craft or cooking class. Be on the lookout when you take walks in the neighborhood. Watch for the potential of new friendships when you go on your child's field trip, help out with the school play, share carpool duties, or work as a homeroom mom. Not every connection you make will become a lifelong bond, but you never know when a true, lasting sisterhood might be born.

The Bible tells the story of two women who developed a wonderful friendship through their common bond of faith in Christ. Perhaps you are familiar with their names: Mary Magdalene and Mary the mother of James and Joses. But have you ever pondered the beauty of their sisterhood? These faithful women experienced the most significant events of their lives (and all of history) together.

Mary Magdalene was the first person to see Christ's empty tomb and the first to report the resurrection to the disciples. She was the first one to speak to the resurrected Jesus. What a high honor! Commentators since the Middle Ages have attempted to identify her as the woman with a sinful past who anointed Jesus with oil in Luke 7:36–50, but there is no evidence to support that claim. The name "Magdalene" is derived from Magdala, her hometown south of the Plain of Gennesaret. Most likely Mary was one of the influential women of Magdala. We do know that she was a devoted follower with a heart of profound gratitude, since we are told in Scripture that Jesus healed her of seven demons (Mark 16:9).

Mary the mother of James and Joses was another one of Jesus' faithful followers. She is introduced to us at the cross in Matthew 27:55–56: "Many women were there [the crucifixion], watching from a distance. They had followed Jesus from Galilee to care for his needs. Among them were Mary Magdalene, Mary the mother of James and Joses, and the mother of Zebedee's sons." This second Mary (also called the wife of Clopas in John 19:25) served Jesus in the hour of his greatest need. She brought sweet spices to Christ's tomb to anoint his body (Mark 16:1), and along with Mary Magdalene, found the tomb empty and reported the good news to the apostles.

We don't know when these women first met, but we do know what brought them together: a common bond of faith in Jesus. A common goal to serve him. A common grief at his death. A common joy at his resurrection. No doubt their sisterhood was cemented through the events they experienced together. It's lovely to think about how these women must have encouraged one another in their faith, especially after Jesus ascended into heaven. Despite their different backgrounds and walks of life, these two Marys discovered and nurtured a significant and meaningful connection.

Building on Common Interests

What are some of the ways we connect with other people? Let's think intentionally for a moment about the common bonds that can take an acquaintance friendship to the next level. Certainly spiritual bonds—the kind that connected the two Marys—are at the top of any list. Spiritual bonds are so significant, in fact, that we've written an entire chapter (chapter 12) on them. Here are some other common interests we can build friendships upon:

Hobbies

"What? You love scrapbooking? So do I! Let's get together and work on ours." A potential friendship is born! Hobbies offer a wonderful basis for not only friendship, but fun. Whether you love gourmet cooking or quilting or painting pottery, keep an open ear and eye for those who share your interest. Go ahead, you be the one to get the friendship started. Plan a day to work on your hobby and creatively craft together.

Sports

Are you a walker or a jogger? Usually you'll find that people are one of the two. We all could use a little exercise, so why not plan to meet someone for a walk or jog through the neighborhood? Or ask a new friend to play tennis, golf, softball, or soccer with you. Go skeet shooting together or lift weights. Build that muscle while you're building your friendship.

Theatrical Interests

The theater, the theater, everyone loves the theater! You may be a moviegoer or a play watcher. Or maybe the opera is your cup of tea. Enjoy the show with someone else, and set the stage for a new relationship.

Volunteerism

Serving others brings women together. If you are lonely, volunteer for a committee at school or in a local charity. You're likely to find a new friend and be a blessing along the way. Consider serving in politics; your party needs you! Help out on a church committee or at a city event. You will be surprised at the number of acquaintances who will turn into wonderful friends.

Books

Did you see a woman reading a book by your favorite author? Then read between the lines: You have something in common! You may want to exchange books or get together over coffee and discuss a book you agree to read at the same time. Book a date right now to go to the local bookstore and find your next selection together.

The Visual Arts

Do you know someone who is as impressed with impressionism as you are? Maybe you have discovered another art enthusiast! Schedule a trip to a local art museum or be on the lookout for an exhibit coming to your area. Invite your new friend to enjoy an afternoon of cultural refinement as you draw on your common interests.

Business Bonds

Perhaps you and several other women have the basic foundation of working for the same company or in the same building. Circumstances have put you together; and if you are willing, you can build friendships on that common business bond. Watch to see whom you naturally gravitate toward as you and your coworkers talk and share information about your lives.

Of course, these are not the only bonds that connect people. The things we might find in common with other women are too numerous to mention here. We've simply listed these few to stimulate your thinking about the potential friendships that exist all around you. The important thing is not so much that you discover common interests, but rather that you do something with them. Are you willing to be the one to make the initial step to reach beyond the acquaintance circle and start a good friendship?

A Difficult Bond

It's fun to think about the common bonds we share with other women based on hobbies, interests, and activities. But sometimes the deepest bonding takes place when we share a tragedy or difficulty with someone else. In fact, the worst of situations can bond people together in ways that good times can't. Take the early Christians, for example.

Under the hand of persecution, their love and care for one another flourished. Their faith in Christ and commitment to each other stood strong in tough times.

Think about 9/11. The bonding of a nation—crossing all political, racial, and social lines—took place through the horrible circumstances of that deadly terrorist attack. The American people stood together, one nation under God, in a way that wouldn't have happened in good times. Not that we wish for tragedy; but if it takes place, the bonding of people in the aftermath can provide a glimmer of sunshine and hope.

In 2 Corinthians 1:3–7, Paul speaks of the comfort we can bring to others through the common bond of suffering:

> Praise be to the God and Father of our Lord Jesus Christ, the Father of compassion and the God of all comfort, who comforts us in all our troubles, so that we can comfort those in any trouble with the comfort we ourselves have received from God. For just as the sufferings of Christ flow over into our lives, so also through Christ our comfort overflows. If we are distressed, it is for your comfort and salvation; if we are comforted, it is for your comfort, which produces in you patient endurance of the same sufferings we suffer. And our hope for you is firm, because we know that just as you share in our sufferings, so also you share in our comfort.

Often we wonder why we go through a terrible situation or tragedy. We may never know the full answer this side of heaven. But one thing we do know: We can be compassionate and helpful toward others who are suffering if we ourselves have been through a similar loss or grief.

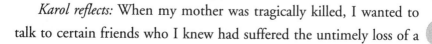

Karol reflects: When my mother was tragically killed, I wanted to talk to certain friends who I knew had suffered the untimely loss of a

There is space within sisterhood for likeness and difference, for the subtle differences that challenge and delight; there is space for disappointment—and surprise. —Christine Downing

parent. Somehow it helped me to know that they could relate. Our common tragedy bonded us in a way that we would not have chosen. But we needed each other. Before my mother died, I had not experienced a death in the family. I had no idea how to comfort a friend who was grieving the loss of a loved one. Now I do.

❀　❀　❀

Beth's son, Kurt, was born with Golden Har Syndrome, which meant he had numerous birth defects and faced a multitude of surgeries. While waiting at the hospital during one of Kurt's surgeries, Beth met Susan, whose son, Terry, also had multiple physical challenges. Beth and Susan shared their emotions, struggles, and pain that day. Over the weeks and months that followed, they encouraged one another and helped each other whenever possible. A unique bond was formed between the mothers that still exists today, sixteen years later.

Like Beth and Susan, we often discover wonderful heart friendships when we're going through difficult times. That's not the way we would choose to begin a friendship; but then, when do we need a friend more? When tragedy strikes, don't isolate yourself. Instead, look for people God places in your path who have gone down the road before you. Later, when you are able to assist someone else down a similarly rough road, make yourself available. Friendships born of compassion are lasting and true.

A Delightful Pursuit

Have you had the opportunity to meet Anne of Green Gables? Perhaps you read her story as a young girl. Or maybe you read it to your own children or watched the video. If you have met her, then you know that *Anne of Green Gables* by Lucy Maud Montgomery is a heartwarming book about a young, vibrant, redheaded orphan girl who is mistakenly adopted by an elderly couple. (They had requested a boy to work the farm, but Anne was sent to them, instead.) The saga follows Anne's experiences as she overcomes difficulties and learns to control her strong-willed spirit.

In large part, the book is about relationships. Anne places a high value on her friendships. When she finds people she can connect with, she gives them the blessed status of "kindred spirits." Anne comes to have many kindred spirits; yet she longs for a soul mate—that closest and dearest of friends. She finally finds that "heart friend" in Diana. The two girls share their most intimate secrets, hopes, dreams, dreads, and fears. They are bonded as sisters for life, and nothing can come against them.

We can all take a few cues from Anne. She kept her eyes wide open for those aha moments when an acquaintance passed into her circle of kindred spirits. These friends were treasures indeed! And then, with deliberate determination, she discovered her soul-mate friend. She valued, supported, and encouraged Diana through thick and thin. Anne had a ready eye to see the many potential friendships in her life—and a willing heart to nurture those friendships with deep devotion.

We, too, can develop new friends out of our pool of acquaintances. We can find that special soul mate who will stick with us through thick and thin. All we need is that same ready eye and willing heart that Anne had.

Go ahead. Put up your "friendship antennas" so you can detect those relationships that have the greatest potential. Then take intentional steps to build on the common bonds you discover. As the saying goes, "If it is to be, it is up to me." Be a positive friend—and positive friends will surely find you.

POWER POINT

⚙ **Read:** Mark 15:40; 16:11. Picture these women as they walked to the tomb with their spices, discussing what they were going to do about the stone in front of the tomb. What do you think they said to one another? What do you think they said or did on the way back to tell the disciples the good news? Do you have a friend with whom you have bonded together through sorrow and joy?

♡ **Pray:** Precious and wonderful heavenly Father, I praise you for the blessing of friends. Thank you for the sisters you have brought into my life through the common bonds of friendship. Help me to recognize aha moments when they happen, and give me the wisdom to build on them. Please lead new people into my life with whom I can connect. Bless my friendships and help them to grow and develop in quality and depth through the years. Thank you for being my closest of friends. In Jesus' name, amen.

💡 **Remember:** "Let brotherly love continue" (Hebrews 13:1 KJV).

☺ **Do:** Write down the names of some of the acquaintances in your life right now. Pray and ask God to show you someone on the list with whom you might have a common bond. Consider ways you can build on that bond, and take the first step toward making it happen.

Woman to Woman
The Beauty of Friendships throughout the Ages

*I have learned that to have a good friend is the purest of all God's gifts,
for it is a love that has no exchange of payment.*

—Frances Farmer

Picture this: It's Saturday night. You are home alone. Your house is spotless—not a dish in the sink, not a towel left to be folded. Even your junk drawer in the kitchen has been cleaned out and organized. Outside your window, snow is sleepily drifting down. You snuggle up on the couch in your comfiest pajamas, hot chocolate in hand, and prepare to watch back-to-back episodes of the greatest rerun of all time: *I Love Lucy.*

Doesn't just thinking about such a night make you smile? We can't help but laugh out loud when we reflect on some of the most memorable Lucy-and-Ethel moments that have entertained us over the years. The two friends always seemed to find themselves together in the middle of a mess that most of us could relate to. Whether it was making one too many purchases, slipping the packages into the closet and bringing them out one by one over time to keep the hubby happy or simply opening their mouths and inserting a foot one too many times, their messes were our messes too. We all came to feel an affinity and affection for this special duo.

But think about it: How did Lucy and Ethel make their way into our hearts? What was it about their rapport with one another that struck a chord with us?

Lucy and Ethel didn't have a perfect friendship, if only for the mere fact that these two gal pals were far from perfect people. Lucy—spontaneous, scattered, daring, and brash—was forever roping Ethel into one of her mischievous schemes and drawing her friend far out of her comfort zone. Meanwhile, Ethel—methodical, organized, cautious, and timid—tended to look at life from the perspective that the glass is always half empty, and therefore she often rained on Lucy's parade. But what a blessed balance they were for one another!

Not that Lucy ever really heeded any of Ethel's warnings. As Lucy would recklessly lead the way toward her objective, determined to get what she wanted, Ethel would forever be the trooper, following loyally behind, and more often than not, helping Lucy out of a pickle. Truly these two friends were committed to one another. And truly their lives were made richer because of that commitment as they shared joys, griefs, embarrassing moments, and misguided adventures.

There is something unique and glorious about the ties that bind the hearts of women together. These ties come in varying lengths, strengths, colors, and materials. They have to. We are all so different. Even though Lucy and Ethel happened to be about the same age, their personalities were dramatically opposite, and they needed a unique tie that took their differences into account.

Age, race, marital status, career choice, and personality do not limit friendships between women. Many times we bond with one another, not because we are alike, but because we are able to meet a need in each other's lives. Just as Lucy and Ethel provided emotional balance for one another, our closest friends oftentimes "round us out." They complete us in a special way, providing strength in the areas where we are weak. Such positive friendships are rare and valuable. And they are available to us all.

A Friendship Journey

Reflecting on the beauty of friendships throughout history encourages us to value and strengthen the bonds of sisterhood in our own lives. It teaches us how and why certain types of relationships work. So let's journey back to ancient days to begin our friendship travels. Along the way, let's keep our eyes open for the life-changing ways in which positive friendships between women have impacted our world.

Biblical Friends

The Bible contains many beautiful stories about friendship between women. In the last chapter we looked at the bond of sisterhood between the two Marys, who found themselves together because of their common faith in Christ.

During a dark time in Israel's history, there glimmered a precious light of friendship. The story actually begins during a severe famine in the land of Judah. A man named Elimelech from Bethlehem took his wife and two sons to live in the country of Moab. The two sons married Moabite girls. Unfortunately, it was only a matter of time before Elimelech and his sons died leaving the two Moabite girls with their mother-in-law, Naomi. As the three headed back to Judah, Naomi stopped and told the girls to go back to their families. The three of them broke down and wept, as they didn't want to part company.

One of the girls, Ruth, decided to stay with Naomi. It was here that Ruth made one of the most beautiful pledges of loyalty in history. "Don't ask me to leave you and turn back. I will go wherever you go and live wherever you live. Your people will be my people, and your God will be my God. I will die where you die and will be buried there. May the LORD punish me severely if I allow anything but death to separate us!" (Ruth 1:16–17 NLT). From that moment on, a devoted friendship shined brightly between the two women.

Ruth and Naomi encouraged and helped one another as they made their home in Bethlehem. God gave Ruth a wonderful new husband named Boaz. Soon they had a baby, and Naomi lovingly stayed close and cared for the baby as if he were her own. It's easy to see that Ruth and Naomi were bonded through their selfless loyalty and loving care for one another. Even the women of the town noticed the special bond between the two. They described Ruth as the daughter-in-law who loves Naomi and "has been better to you than seven sons" (Ruth 4:15 NLT). One could probably say, "Marriage made them in-laws; loyal devotion made them friends."

Now let's go to the first chapter of Luke—a chapter we tend to think of as dealing with the heavenly birth announcements of John the Baptist and Jesus. But as we take another look at this passage of Scripture, we discover that it also has to do with a history-defining friendship between two women.

Mary and Elizabeth were cousins from different towns who both found themselves in extraordinary pregnancies at about the same time. Elizabeth was quite old and had been barren for years; yet God chose her to be the mother of John the Baptist, the prophet who would prepare the way for Jesus. Mary, on the other hand, was very young and a virgin; yet God chose her to bear his Son. The two women were much more than relatives to one another. They were soul mates, because they shared a deep and unique bond: Each woman carried a miracle child.

Let's observe the account of their greeting found in Luke 1:39–45:

At that time Mary got ready and hurried to a town in the hill country of Judea, where she entered Zechariah's home and greeted Elizabeth. When Elizabeth heard Mary's greeting, the baby leaped in her womb, and Elizabeth was filled with the Holy Spirit. In a loud voice she exclaimed: "Blessed are you among women, and blessed is the child you will bear! But why am I so favored, that the mother of my Lord should come to me? As soon as the sound of your greeting reached my ears, the baby in my womb leaped for joy. Blessed is she who has believed that what the Lord has said to her will be accomplished!"

What a prophetic blessing Elizabeth spoke to Mary! She didn't say one discouraging word, even though Mary's pregnancy was probably a public scandal. Instead, words of encouragement poured across Elizabeth's lips directly from God's heart. Whenever doubt entered Mary's mind as she carried the Christ child to term, all she had to do was remember back to her cousin's greeting to be reminded of God's purpose and faithfulness toward her.

According to Luke 1:56, Mary and Elizabeth actually lived together under one roof for several months. (Don't you feel sorry for Elizabeth's husband, Zechariah? He had two hormonal women to care for at the same time!) When Mary came to live with her cousin, she was in her first trimester, and Elizabeth was in her last. No doubt the two women were able to empathize with one another about the normal discomforts of pregnancy. Morning sickness, swollen ankles, lower back pain, and an overall sense of perpetual tiredness probably plagued them both.

On top of their physical struggles, both women had to deal with the unwanted stares and judgmental gossip of acquaintances, friends, and family. Can't you hear the tongues wagging?

"Can you believe it? That old couple is finally going to have a baby! The poor child—everyone will think his *grandparents* have come to watch his soccer games!"

"What a scandal! The old priest and his wife have taken in their wayward niece. She's pregnant, you know. I heard her fiancé is devastated. He claims he's not the father. He should do what the law allows and stone her to death!"

"She always seemed like such a nice girl. But the truth about your character always finds you out. What a disgrace."

Both of these precious women were willing to be used by God in ways that would ultimately change the future for all mankind. But it wasn't going to be easy for them. Although God's plan for us is always perfect, it's not always an easy road to travel. Thankfully, God is faithful to equip us physically, mentally, spiritually, and emotionally for the journey. How loving he is! He knew full well what Mary and Elizabeth would go through. He knew they would need each other.

When the angel came to Mary and told her that she would be giving birth, Mary was troubled and perplexed, asking, "How will this be, since I am a virgin?"

The angel explained in Luke 1:35, "The Holy Spirit will come upon you, and the power of the Most High will overshadow you. So the holy one to be born will be called the Son of God."

Then the angel went on to answer more than the question she had asked aloud. He knew that she had other questions, deeper questions, in her heart. Surely she was thinking, *How will I ever get through this?* In his tenderness, God directed the angel to give Mary this additional piece of good news: "Even Elizabeth your relative is going to have a child in her old age, and she who was said to be barren is in her sixth month. For nothing is impossible with God" (Luke 1:36–37). God had given Mary a friend to help her bear the burden!

From that point on, these two friends were able to share the joy of knowing that they were co-laborers (quite literally, if you'll pardon the pun!) with the God of the universe. Certainly, they helped one another with the physically exhausting and sometimes mundane aspects of running a household. But even more importantly, they supported one another and encouraged one another during the difficult days. They lifted each other's spirits by sharing both the struggles and joys that come with life. May we all find friends so dear!

An Unmatched Commitment

There is probably no greater friendship to be found in American history than that of Helen Keller (1880–1968) and her devoted teacher and friend, Anne Mansfield Sullivan (1866–1936). Although partially blind herself, Anne taught Helen (who lost her sight and hearing before she was two years old) with an unmatched dedication and love. Through the sense of touch, she opened Helen's world to life and learning. Helen eventually enrolled in prep school and college, graduating from Radcliff University in 1904. Their abiding friendship continued until Anne's death.

Why did Helen and Anne bond so deeply? *Commitment.* Deep within the bonds of sisterhood is always a giving of oneself completely to the other person. Anne dedicated herself to the betterment of Helen Keller and brought a new light to Helen's world. Helen's eyes may have remained blinded; but thanks to Anne, she didn't have to live with a mind that was in darkness or a spirit that was in

Two are better than one, because they have a good return for their work: If one falls down, his friend can help him up. But pity the man who falls and has no one to help him up! —Ecclesiastes 4:9–10

bondage. And their friendship was not a one-way street. Helen brought purpose, meaning, and fulfillment to Anne Sullivan's life. May each of us enrich our lives and the lives of others through dedicated and committed friendships!

Sisters in Work

Corrie ten Boom (1892–1983) was a Dutch woman who, along with her family, opened her home as a refuge for Jews during World War II. Her bravery and sacrifice landed her in a German concentration camp, where her faith in God saw her through much pain and fear. Her story is told in the best-selling novel *The Hiding Place* by John and Elizabeth Sherrill, which later became a popular movie by the same name.

After the war "Tante Corrie," as she was lovingly called (*Tante* is the Dutch word for "Aunt"), began speaking all over the world, relating what God had taught her during her years of incarceration. In 1976 her ministry was still going strong, despite the fact that she was no longer a tall, young brunette but rather a stooped, silver-haired, eighty-three-year-old woman with a weak heart. Now, because of her age, health, and work schedule, she needed someone to help her.

Through a series of events and God's perfect timing, a young, single woman of thirty-two entered Corrie's life. Pam Rosewell Moore, more than fifty years Corrie ten Boom's junior, took the job and title of "companion" in order to further the ministry God had planned not only for Corrie but for Pam as well. Pam came to Corrie after having been the personal assistant to Brother Andrew, the author of the well-known Christian book *God's Smuggler*. Brother Andrew spent many years smuggling Bibles into Iron Curtain countries, and Pam had been privileged to assist him for seven of those years. Now Pam had a new assignment. But God had more in store for her relationship with Corrie than a mere work association.

❀

Terry Ann reflects: I have been privileged to know Pam Rosewell Moore as a friend and colleague at Dallas Baptist University, and I've had the joy of listening to her talk about her special relationship with Corrie ten Boom. Here is what Pam once told me in her soft-spoken, delightful British dialect about their treasured friendship:

> Tante Corrie was a strong Dutch woman, and one characteristic of the Dutch is that you always know where you stand with them. Tante Corrie was very straightforward, and at times that was difficult for me.
>
> I must tell you, it's not always easy taking on the role of servant. I did not set out to be the companion and assistant to an elderly woman. I had desires of my own to be married and raise a family. But the Lord knew best.
>
> Over time, our relationship changed. It became a friendship. I could serve Corrie freely because she was my friend. And Corrie was truly interested in me. She wanted God's best for my life; so even though I had a subservient role to play, I always knew that she viewed me as equally important in the work we did for the Lord.
>
> Some people saw me as someone who lived in the shadow of the very famous Corrie ten Boom. But I knew I was Corrie's confidant. She trusted me with her thoughts and confidential stories from her past. As I typed her manuscript that became the best-selling devotional *Each New Day*, she asked me, "Have I covered everything important?" I felt she might need to include more information about God's grace. She seriously pondered my suggestion and then went straight away to make the additions.

She was not too proud to allow the one who served her to make suggestions regarding her work.

Through our relationship I learned what real friendship and loyalty is about. I was with Corrie during her 'quiet years' after her stroke, leading up to her death in 1983. At times the days and months seemed to last forever as I cared for her during her long illness. I came to enjoy blessing Tante Corrie by rubbing her feet and painting her nails. I realized that in that act of service towards my friend was an act of worship to my Lord.

❖ ❖ ❖

What a beautiful example of a positive, affirming, sacrificing friendship! We would all do well to have such a friend—or be such a friend.

What We Know about Girlfriends

Every once in a while you receive an e-mail that sticks with you. Here's one that we really like. Sadly, we don't know who to attribute these profound words to. But they speak marvelously to the essence of friendships between "us girls":

> I sat under a tree in the hot sun on a summer day, drinking iced tea and getting to know my new sister-in-law. Not much older than I, but already the mother of three, she seemed to me to be experienced and wise. "Get yourself some girlfriends," she advised, clinking the ice cubes in her glass. "You are going to need girlfriends. Go places with them; do things with them."
>
> *What a funny piece of advice,* I thought. Hadn't I just gotten married? Hadn't I just joined the couple-world? I was a married woman, for goodness sakes, not a young girl who needed girlfriends. But I listened to this new sister-in-law. I got myself some

girlfriends. And as the years tumbled by, one after another, gradually I came to understand that she knew what she was talking about. Here's what I know about girlfriends:

- Girlfriends bring casseroles and scrub your bathroom when you are sick.

- Girlfriends keep your children and keep your secrets.

- Girlfriends give advice when you ask for it. Sometimes you take it; sometimes you don't.

- Girlfriends don't always tell you that you're right, but they're usually honest.

- Girlfriends still love you, even when they don't agree with your choices.

- Girlfriends might send you a birthday card, but they might not. It doesn't matter in the least.

- Girlfriends laugh with you, and you don't need canned jokes to start the laughter.

- Girlfriends pull you out of jams.

- Girlfriends don't keep a calendar that lets them know who hosted the other last.

- Girlfriends are there for you, in an instant and truly, when the hard times come.

- Girlfriends listen when you lose a job or a husband.

- Girlfriends listen when your children break your heart.

- Girlfriends listen when your parents' minds and bodies fail.

- My girlfriends bless my life. Once we were young, with no idea of the incredible joys or the incredible sorrows that lay ahead. Nor did we know how much we would need each other.[1]

This e-mail writer got it right. Lucy and Ethel would thoroughly agree! We all need positive friends.

The truth is, friendships between women don't just happen. Friends may seem to come into our lives by accident, but that's never the case. True friends are a gift from God. Our heavenly Father's desire is for us to have meaningful and soul-nurturing friendships with other women, because he knows that friends support, encourage, bless, and serve one another in ways no one else can.

God gave Mary her Elizabeth. He gave Helen Keller her Anne Sullivan and Corrie ten Boom her Pam Rosewell Moore. We can be sure that if we ask him, he will bring wonderful, positive friends into our lives too.

POWER POINT

⚙ **Read:** Luke 1. Reflect on the friendship between Elizabeth and Mary. What aspects about their relationship did you notice that perhaps you never saw before? Has God given you a friendship like this?

♥ **Pray:** O glorious and wonderful Father, you are my provider and my helper. Thank you for the unique qualities you have given to me as a woman. May I use them to build deeper and more abiding relationships with others! Thank you for the friends and kindred spirits you have brought and will bring into my life. Help me to be an encouragement and a blessing to them. Teach me to be a devoted and committed friend. Help me to be willing to step out of my comfort zone in order to be a friend to those who are different from me. In Jesus' name I pray, amen.

💡 **Remember:** "Two are better than one, because they have a good return for their work" (Ecclesiastes 4:9).

☺ **Do:** Draw a timeline of your life, indicating major events from birth to the present. Who were your good friends and soul mates during your school years? What about after high school? Who are your friends today? As you reflect back over the friends God has brought into your life, thank him for these special people. Pray for the needs in their lives right now, wherever they may be. Pick one person that you will try to contact either by phone or mail to let her know that you were thinking about her. Tell her that you're thankful for her friendship.

Power Principle #2

THe Power oF encouragement

*Pleasant words to others can have a permanent,
even eternal, impact for good.*

—Kenneth Parlin

Man's highest duty is to encourage others.

—Chuck Swindoll

Cheerleaders
Being Your Friend's Biggest Fan

There are so many hurts that circumstances and the world inflict upon us, we need the constant reinforcement of encouragement.

—Billy Graham

Two, four, six, eight, who do we appreciate? Friends! Friends! Friends!

Everyone needs a few good cheerleaders. When we were children, we ate up our parents' applause: "You can do it. You're doing a great job! We're so pleased with you!" Now we are grown, and our parents aren't always there to offer their accolades. That's where positive friends step in.

There is not a person alive who doesn't need a positive friend. We all need to feel valued and appreciated by someone. We all need to be cheered on in our life's journey. But sadly, this need goes unmet in many of our lives. As we speak to women's groups around the country on the topic of friendship, we hear one consistent plea. Women everywhere tell us, "I want someone who will build me up, laugh with me, and encourage me. I want a positive friend."

A positive friend is someone who encourages us—who sees who we are, notices the things we do, and says, "You go, girl." That encouragement is so critical to our souls that some of us will go to great lengths to get it.

Terry Ann reflects: Take me, for instance. Let me begin by stating that I am married to a terrific guy. I fell in love with my six-foot-five-inch, blue-eyed, blond-haired, muscle-clad hunk when we were both twenty-six. Now wouldn't you know that God, in all his wisdom and humor, would arrange for this strong, silent-type man of few words to fall in love with a woman who makes her living using her gift of gab as a public speaker and radio talk-show host? I like to express myself freely and often; and what's more, as a former communications instructor on a college campus, I taught others to do the same! All that to say, I've thrown myself a little pity party at different times in our married life. I've felt that Jay didn't appreciate me, because he found it so difficult to tell me specifically the qualities he saw and admired in me.

It took years, but finally I came up with a solution to prevent my emotional marital meltdowns. Jay and I had gone away for the weekend to celebrate our fourteenth anniversary. Everything was perfect: great weather, no kids, great hotel, no kids, great restaurants, no kids, great relaxation, no kids. There was only one thing missing. I longed to hear Jay whisper sweet nothings in my ear, but all I got was the "nothing" part.

That's when it hit me. I knew that Jay loved me. All he needed was a little help expressing his encouraging words of affirmation.

I began, "Honey, I really need to know that you are still madly in love with me and that you greatly admire all my tremendously wonderful traits. So I'm going to say what I hope you feel about me, and all you have to say is 'I agree with that.'"

Jay grinned. "Go for it!" he said.

"For a woman in her forties, I look pretty good."

"I agree with that."

"I do a great job managing all five children's schedules."

"I agree with that."

"I have an outgoing and fun personality."

"I agree with that."

"I'm the only woman for you, and you're crazy about me."

"I agree with that."

You get the idea. It was amazing! The more I voiced all the encouraging words I desired to hear from the most significant person in my life, the more loved I felt—simply because he said, "I agree with that!" We had a great laugh, and Jay got the point: Women—no, all people—need meaningful verbal encouragement.

❖ ❖ ❖

Each of us has the ability to offer that kind of affirmation to others. Unfortunately, in our "hurry up, gotta go" world, we often fail to be positive friends. The co-worker who arrives early to make sure we all have coffee in the office, the school teacher who takes extra time after school to tutor our children, the mail carrier who always has a warm smile and a friendly wave as she drops off the mail—all of these are people who need words of positive encouragement just as much as we do, if we would only notice.

It's sad but true that most of us are quick with words of criticism and slow with words of praise. We complain to the restaurant manager when the waitress delivers poor service. But how often do we request to see the manager in order to compliment the employee who went beyond the call of duty to ensure our dining experience was perfect? Why is this? Why is it hard for us to encourage others when we so enjoy receiving encouraging words ourselves? We can give the excuse

He who refreshes others will himself be refreshed. —Proverbs 11:25

"I'm too busy." Then why do we always seem to find the time when we have a complaint? We can say, "I just don't think about it." That's probably closer to the truth.

Let's create a new habit. Let's determine to become women of encouragement—women whose aim it is to cheer from the sidelines as our family and friends engage in the difficult and sometimes discouraging game of life. Being a cheerleader is easier than we might think. The following words found in Cheri Fuller's book *The Fragrance of Kindness* are so true: "It was only a sunny smile, and little it cost in the giving. But like the morning light, it scattered the night, and made the day worth living!"[1]

John Hay once said, "Friends are the sunshine of life."[2] Positive friends bring light to our lives and strength to our souls through their encouragement and love. They are a refreshment to us, not a drain.

Encourager or Discourager?

Have you ever noticed that certain friends in your life make you feel like a better person when you're with them? Maybe it's the way they smile at you or the kind words they say; something about them makes their presence in your life a constant source of encouragement and blessing. Unfortunately, not all friends have that same effect. You probably have other friends, who when you're with them, seem to suck the life right out of you. Maybe it's their constant complaining or the way they look at you. Their words and demeanor, more often than not, express judgment rather than acceptance, and you leave their presence feeling tired and deflated.

Take a minute to reflect on your inner circle of friends. As you make a mental picture of each of them, ask yourself: If I were building a house, would they be on my building crew or my demolition crew? Builders look at a project—in this case, you—and see endless possibilities. They see the beauty that already exists and the potential that lies within. The folks on the demolition crew, on the other hand, don't care about beauty; their focus is on what is wrong and needs changing. They are ready and willing to point out how you could have done something different or better. People on the demolition crew are always complaining about something. Somehow, instead of making lemonade from lemons, they always end up sucking on the lemons!

A Builder Friend

Beth is a builder friend. When you call her up, she's always glad to hear from you—even though you know she is knee-deep in laundry and preschoolers. You can almost hear her smile over the phone through her tone of voice. She is a true encourager. Every conversation is saturated with kind and uplifting thoughts. She admonishes when necessary and gently lets you know when she doesn't agree with your actions, all the while covering her words with love, concern, and kindness.

She is the type that when you have a new idea, she's for it. She may give you suggestions, but they are quite welcome since you are convinced she has your best interests at heart. Beth not only has good words for you; she also speaks good words about your family. She is well aware that your husband and kids are not perfect, yet she can always find good things to say that help you see your loved ones in the best light.

❖

Karol reflects: Beth recently said this to me about my daughter: "Grace just lights up the room with her smile. She makes everyone feel important, as if they were the only person in the room." This comment couldn't have come at a better time, since Grace had been feeling rather low in confidence. When I passed on Beth's compliment, Grace's spirits were lifted. My dear builder friend brought me just the right verbal building blocks when I needed them!

✿ ✿ ✿

A Demolition Friend

Debbie (not her real name) is your typical discourager. She not only sees the wrong in your life and family, she continually whines and complains about her own life as well. She is not exactly what you would call refreshment to your soul! When you see her number show up on Caller ID, you think twice about answering. In a typical conversation with her, you hear all over again how everything is wrong in her life and in the lives of her family members. She also makes sure you know about the frailties of other women in your circle of friends and acquaintances.

Instead of having eyes that look up at hope and eternal potential, her eyes look down at potential hazards and miseries. When it is sunshiny outside, it's too hot and muggy. When it is cloudy outside, it's too gloomy, and rain is surely on the way. Whereas Beth Builder would call up and say, "Isn't it a beautiful day!" Debbie Demolition would call and ask you to pray for cloud cover, because she's going to be outside at the zoo on a field trip with her kids, and she doesn't want it to be too hot. She is forever finding fault with the school and the teacher, the church and the preacher.

Don't misunderstand. We're not saying that constructive criticism has no value. Where would we be if it weren't for people down through history who were discontent with the status quo? We all benefit when someone is willing to correct or point out a legitimate problem. But attitude is everything! Cheerleaders cheer even when the team is behind. As a matter of fact, that is when they cheer the loudest!

Demolition Dominoes

A few years ago, a local television station filmed and later aired the demolition of an older high-rise office building in our area. It was amazing to watch the large wrecking ball as it swung from the crane and delivered the first fatal blow to the magnificent old structure. You could actually see the building begin to crumble immediately upon impact. Unlike a building destroyed by dynamite—*kaboom,* and it's gone—a wrecking ball gets the destruction process started. Then the domino effect takes over and completes the job. Whether by dynamite or by wrecking ball, the end result is still the same: a destroyed structure.

In a way, that's how negative friends affect those around them. Over a period of time, they emotionally tear away or wear away the once-positive morale that existed between friends and family. They can even harm organizations such as churches, Bible studies, and schools. What may begin as the throwing of a few small stones can result in the complete crumbling of individual friendships or organizational relationships. What's left behind in the rubble? The debris of broken trust, destroyed reputations, and shattered friendships.

You can read about some heavy-duty discouragers in the Bible. In Numbers 16, we find that Moses was doing his best to perform the difficult job God gave him of leading the Israelite people. Along came Korah, Dathan, and Abiram, "friends" who were insolent and discontented. They decided to rise up against Moses. They even rounded up 250 others and passed on their lynch-mob mentality to them! These three "friends" bragged about being holy and questioned Moses'

Rejoice with them that do rejoice, and weep with them that weep. —Romans 12:15 KJV

71

authority. Fortunately, Moses truly desired God's holiness and cried out to the Lord about their complaints—something Korah, Dathan, and Abiram should have considered.

How did God view their complaints? How did he view the divisiveness these three "friends" caused among the people? To put it bluntly, he was not pleased, and they were consumed by fire.

These three are not the only Bible characters who knew how to rain on someone's parade. The Scripture is full of demolition experts, from those "friends" who discouraged Job, to those who discouraged Nehemiah, to those who tried to trip up Jesus. Most of these naysayers probably didn't even realize they were being negative! That just goes to show that we must continually check our attitude and actions to make sure we are being builders and uplifters, not demolishers and discouragers.

When Encouragement Is Needed the Most

We want to be the kind of women who cheer others on in the course of their life journeys. The question is, for whom do we cheer? Do we only applaud those who are doing well, who are succeeding in some aspect of life? Definitely, we should try to point out the good we see in every life that touches ours. However, there are two special groups of people who need our encouragement the most: those who are without hope and those who have been misunderstood.

Encouragement for the Misunderstood

Barnabas was a builder friend for the apostle Paul. His very name means "encourager." We meet Barnabas in Acts 9, just after Paul (known at the time as Saul) had his dramatic encounter with Christ on the road to Damascus. Paul's conversion to Christianity was hard for some disciples to believe, and understandably so. Acts 9:1 tells us that before his Damascus Road experience, "Saul was still breathing out murderous threats against the Lord's disciples." Apparently, Paul had gained quite the reputation. He was famous (or should we say, infamous) in those parts. His resumé included some heavy-duty infractions—such as persecuting and killing people for their belief in Christ as the Messiah.

We can certainly understand why many of the early Christians were a bit leery of Paul, to put it mildly. Was his "conversion" simply a strategic tactic to lure in believers so he could then hand them over to the Jewish authorities? In Acts 9:13 we read the response of Ananias, a Christian follower, when God told him to go to Saul and pray for him: "'Lord,' Ananias answered, 'I have heard many reports about this man and all the harm he has done to your saints in Jerusalem. And he has come here with authority from the chief priests to arrest all who call on your name.'"

Can you blame Ananias for not wanting to throw out the welcome mat when Paul came to town? But God spoke to Ananias and reassured him that Paul's conversion was genuine. Paul ended up spending several days with the disciples in Damascus, preaching, teaching, and leading many to Christ.

It didn't take long for the Jewish leaders to have their fill of the new Paul, however, and they conspired to kill him. He fled to Jerusalem, hoping to join the disciples there. He must have been at least a little concerned about the reception he would get. He was probably thinking, *OK, God, I'll go to Jerusalem. But I hope you have a plan, because the Christians there are going to be out for blood. After all, I've inflicted pain and suffering on many of their family members and friends.*

The world-impacting ministry of Paul could have been very short-lived indeed had it not been for an encourager who came into Paul's life at this critical juncture: Barnabas. As one of the Christian leaders in Jerusalem, Barnabas was able to look at Paul and see past the murderer he had been. He saw Paul in a different light—the new light of Christ. How meaningful this must have been to Paul! He had changed, and he needed someone to see him with new eyes. He needed someone to view him from God's perspective.

As Paul approached Jerusalem, he must have been thinking, *Who will be the one to step out in faith and stand side by side with me? Who will be the one willing to defend me to others so that I can go forward with a new lease on life?* His answer was Barnabas, the encourager.

Acts 9:26–27 tells us, "When he [Paul] came to Jerusalem, he tried to join the disciples, but they were all afraid of him, not believing that he really was a disciple. But Barnabas took him and brought him to the apostles. He told them how Saul on his journey had seen the Lord and that the Lord had spoken to him, and how in Damascus he had preached fearlessly in the name of Jesus."

Instead of seeing Paul's past sins and mistakes, Barnabas saw Paul as a new creation—one that God could use for a great purpose. He overlooked Paul's problematic past and believed in his potential.

No doubt Barnabas was an encourager because he stayed in tune with God. He didn't look at people from man's perspective. "Man looks at the outward appearance, but the LORD looks at the heart," we read in 1 Samuel 16:7. We can assume that Barnabas, like Ananias, had "godly eyes" that were able to see beyond the surface of Paul's life to the God-given potential inside.

What about you? Do you have godly eyes that see past the muck and mire of people's lives? Can you see God's power and potential at work instead? (Aren't you thankful that God looks at *us* that way?)

The fact is, as we walk close with God each day, we begin to see things differently. We begin to see things from an eternal perspective and a hopeful point of view instead of a despairing one. But we must do more than see with godly eyes. We must then act upon what we see.

74

We must take the next step and encourage the ones who have been misunderstood by standing by them and defending them, just as Barnabas did for Paul.

Maybe you can encourage them with these humorous but true words: "You are going to meet your Maker having been misunderstood by someone, so get over it!" Over the course of our lives, all of us are going to be misunderstood by someone sometime. No matter how hard we try to explain, no matter how much we apologize and ask for forgiveness, certain people will never understand. They have once and for all made up their minds about us.

Some of us can simply shrug our shoulders and move on, knowing in our hearts that we did all we could to right the situation. Others of us, though, find it extremely difficult to know we've been misunderstood. We will go to great lengths to rectify a misunderstanding, to no avail. We must take comfort—and encourage our misunderstood friends to take comfort—in the truth that God knows our hearts. He understands, even if everyone else doesn't.

Let's be positive friends and reach out to the woman in the neighborhood, office, or church who is different, whose past may not be as clean, as honorable, as "acceptable" as the others in our group (or, Lord forbid, our clique). Who knows, the one we go out on a limb for, the one we defend and cheer for, may just be the one God has chosen to do a mighty work for him!

Encouragement for the Hopeless

If any woman needs an encourager—a positive builder friend—she's the one who wakes up in the morning and lays her head down each night with an overwhelming sense that life is futile. Hopeless thoughts flood her heart and mind, crippling her ability to perform even simple tasks as she struggles for a sense of purpose. Have you ever felt the pain of hopelessness? Do you know someone who even at this very moment has lost her zeal for living because her life is filled with grief, fear, or pain?

Jeannie Patterson, a vivacious mother and grandmother, has known firsthand the emotion of hopelessness. She also knows the peace and encouragement that comes from God through a positive friend—one who becomes the hands and heart of the Lord, minister to emotional and physical needs. Here's the story Jeannie told us:

I had survived the hardest battle of my life: breast cancer. The Lord and I had won, and it was over. I was at such a good place in my life. I was a divorced mother of four grown children....The Lord had seen me through some difficult days in the past. Now I was living my dream. Having gone back to school later in life, I had completed my second degree in family counseling and was teaching at a wonderful Christian school. I had a private counseling practice as well. I loved spending time with my children and grandbabies....Life was so good.

But then the news came. It was back. My life once again was dark. How would I survive this time? I had no resources left (or so I was convinced) to mount the emotional strength necessary to go toe to toe with the sinister villain of cancer.

My help, my encouragement, came in the form of a friend. Her name is Lori Taylor. Despite being a very busy mother of young children, Lori accompanied me to every single chemotherapy treatment. She made me a priority, even at great personal cost. She put aside her schedule and at times her family in order to help me survive my dungeon of despair. The hope she gave me through her gifts of time and compassion can't be measured. She was even ready to go another round with me if the news came back bad again. The waiting was tough, but thankfully I am now cancer free! I will never forget Lori's selfless love.

Jeannie wrote and dedicated the following poem to Lori (and others like her), who cheered her on during her darkest days:

One Dim Light

Shades of night, blanketed soul,
No stars shine overhead lighting the way.
One dim light flickers
Mouth opened, crying for help
No sound escapes in the blackness.
People without ears
Chain-shackled feet
Laden with burdens; back-breaking load.
Flogged by memories
Bludgeoned heart, tortured mind
No tourniquet to bind the wounds.
Physicians without hands
One dim light shines to bring hope.
One dim light shimmers to call to faith.
One dim light wraps my soul in love.
You, my friend, are that
One dim light.[3]

Who knows when we may be that "one dim light" in someone's life? Lori Taylor knew she was blessing Jeannie, but she never imagined that her act of kindness was the one thing her friend needed in order to keep going. She cheered Jeannie on by sacrificing her time, and in so doing, she brought her friend hope.

Jesus was a giver of hope. He cheered on those the world wrote off. He lifted up those whom the self-righteous labeled as losers. He physically and emotionally healed the sick, the blind, the lame, and the despondent. He made time (and if anyone had lots of important things to do in a day, it was Jesus!) to bring hope.

We can be cheerleaders and hope-givers, too, by the words we say and the things we do. But in order to cheer, we must have something to cheer about. We must look at the people God has placed around us and determine to see the good—the God-potential buried in each one. With godly eyes developed through time spent with the Lord, we must begin to see others as he sees them: unique individuals with endless, positive possibilities.

This may be harder for some of us than for others. Some of us naturally tend to see the glass half empty. But if we will spend time in daily prayer with God and then make a determined, conscious effort to compliment the good we see in the people around us, we will become what we truly want to be: positive, encouraging, hope-giving friends.

POWER POINT

⚙ **Read:** Proverbs 15. Mark every verse that refers to our words or the power of our tongue. What are the traits of a fool's words? Describe a wise man's words.

✌ **Pray:** I praise you, wonderful Father, for you alone are worthy of praise. You are my wonderful redeemer and friend. Your love is perfect, and your power is unmatched. Thank you for making a difference in my life. Thank you for encouraging me. Help me to pour that encouragement out to others, especially my dear friends. Reveal to me opportunities to build others up. Show me specific ways to cheer others on through my words and actions. Pour out your love through me, and let it flow abundantly to those around me. In Jesus' name I pray, amen.

💡 **Remember:** "A man finds joy in giving an apt reply—and how good is a timely word!" (Proverbs 15:23).

☺ **Do:** Think of a friend who could use an uplifting word. Pick up the phone or write her a note, and give her a dose of encouragement. She may need a hug, dinner delivered to her door with a smile, or simply a listening ear. Be that encouragement for her today!

Death at a funeral

Life, Love, and Laughter
Encouraging Ways to Enjoy Your Friendships

Friendship doubles joys and halves griefs.

—Francis Bacon

There's nothing like a good, hearty laugh. As Proverbs 17:22 reminds us, "A cheerful heart is good medicine." It's also the glue that bonds us together as friends.

Friendships between women are not simply about wonderful, enriching conversations (although talking is a big part of friendship for most of us). They are also about enjoying life together. When was the last time you laughed about life with a friend? Perhaps the laughter was prompted by something you chose to do together, like watching a funny movie or going to the fair. Or maybe it erupted from some funny circumstance that just seemed to happen out of nowhere. Whatever the reason, didn't it feel good?

In case you haven't laughed in a while, we want to help you along. Are you ready to laugh?

❖

Terry Ann reflects: I had only run in for one item. Like always, I was in a hurry. And like always, I was running late. It's not that I don't place a value on being punctual; it's just that I think, why waste time? If I

81

have five extra minutes, I might as well be productive. And therein goes the story of my life.

Anyway, in my five extra minutes, I stopped by the grocery store to pick up one item. While I was there, I made a quick dash up and down the aisles, just in case I might discover some unbelievable bargain. And there it was: a lone grocery cart filled to overflowing with canned drinks, with a large sign announcing the price of two six packs for a dollar. Wow! Twelve cans for only one dollar!

I must tell you, I had trouble determining exactly what was in the cans, because the labels were written in Spanish. But once I overcame the language barrier, the news got even better. These were no ordinary canned drinks filled with toxic, nonnutritious, carbonated soda water; they were cans of pure apricot and apple nectar—healthy and probably quite delicious.

I decided I couldn't buy several six packs without trying the drink first, so I picked up a can, popped the lid, and took a swig. (What was the harm? I was going to pay for it.) The flavor was so great that I decided to take them all—the whole cartful.

That's when the store manager, who had been eyeing me as I pondered my good fortune, approached me and offered me a deal I would have been out of my mind to refuse. He had two more carts in the back laden with the same wonderful concoction. He said I could have the whole lot for only twenty dollars. Boy, life is sweet! I said, "Load me up!"

I hurried out to our Suburban and turned it into a cargo van by laying the back seats flat. Then I crammed over 700 cans of Mexican fruit beverage into the car. That's when it hit me: I had to pick up my five children from school in thirty minutes, and now there was no place for them to sit. To make matters worse, half an hour was not nearly enough time to drive home, unload my gold mine, and get to the school.

Thinking quickly, I began making cell phone calls to several friends who lived nearby, offering them home delivery of my wonderful imported refreshments. Then I followed up the phone calls with house calls, unloading the cans in their driveways as I made my way closer and closer to the school. At each stop, my friends and I couldn't help but laugh! One friend's husband turned the delivery into a photo opportunity. I still laugh when I see that picture of my girlfriend Jill and me, smiling as we posed in front of the open doors of my drink-laden SUV.

❖ ❖ ❖

When was the last time you did something fun and frivolous with a friend? Was it last week, last month, last year? Or do you have to think back to your high school or college days? It's sad to think that our lives can get so busy that we fail to have fun! That's not good for us, and it's not good for our friendships.

The key to making a change in the lack-of-fun department is planning. We plan for grocery shopping and bill writing and luncheon meetings; why not make deliberate plans to experience laughter and joy with good friends? This chapter is designed to help you do just that. By the time you finish reading, we hope you are so abundantly blessed with ideas that you will not be able to stop yourself from picking up the phone, calling a friend, and making plans to have fun together.

In the following pages we offer suggestions for different levels of fun. Why different levels? Because the things we might choose to do with an acquaintance-type friend are different than the things we'd choose to do with our closest, dearest gal pals. But the object is the same: to enjoy and deepen our friendships, no matter what level they seem to reflect. Most of the activities we recommend can be enjoyed at any age and take into account a broad cross section of interests, talents, and abilities.

So let's jump right into some serious fun!

Enjoying Acquaintances

Acquaintances are people we see occasionally—for example, at weekly Bible studies, the kids' soccer games, school functions, or committee meetings. We chitchat with them on a surface level. We may or may not know their names. By definition these are not the people we usually make plans to go out and do things with, because if we did, they wouldn't be acquaintances; they would be good friends. And that's the point of this section—to explore ways to enjoy the people we know only casually and hopefully move them to a deeper level of relationship.

Often the first fruits of fellowship begin to bud over a meal together, so consider taking one of these initiatives:

- Invite that fellow soccer mom to join you and your kids after the game for a quick bite to eat.

- Bring in lunch or snacks to the women working with you on that volunteer project.

- After Bible study, invite an acquaintance to meet you for lunch the next day to share prayer requests.

- Instead of eating alone in your cubicle at work, bring in lunch for two from your favorite deli and ask someone you'd like to get to know better to join you.

Another way to develop and deepen new friendships is to get involved at your child's school. At our children's schools, the mothers join together for a major fundraising project each Homecoming. They decorate mums with ribbons and charms and lettering and sell the corsages to the boys to give to their dates for the Homecoming dance. Although it takes hours on end to make these beautiful corsages, the project offers the mothers a wonderful opportunity to get to know each other and share about their lives. Working side by side for hours, the women chat, encourage one another, and get to know more about each other's families. They begin sitting with each other at football games and greeting one another when they pass in the halls at school. Some take the next step and make plans to meet for lunch or shopping. What a fertile ground for friendship!

Ultimately it doesn't matter what activity you choose to share with other women; the important thing is that you devote common time to building a friendship. You don't need to find extra time in your already-busy schedule. You just need to be creative and identify quality time during your normal routine that can be shared with others. Everyone has to eat, right? And if you're going to be sitting in the bleachers at soccer games for the next ten weeks, why not make a friend in the process?

Whatever you do, make a special effort to remember people's names. All of us like nothing better than having our names remembered by someone we've recently met. It makes us feel special and valuable. And keep some good conversation starter questions on the tip of your tongue. That way, when you have a few minutes over a cup of coffee, you won't be at a loss for words. Here are a few open-ended questions or statements to get you started.

- Tell me about your family.

- Where did you grow up?

- How did you first get involved with (or find out about) this church (or school, or soccer team, or job, etc.)?

- What do you like about this organization?

Here's another tip: Keep your eyes and ears open for new friendship opportunities. Paula's recent experience is a good example. She met one of her daughter's new friends, Rebecca, when she drove the girls back to church after they attended a Christian concert. Rebecca had recently moved to the area, so Paula began asking her about her family.

"When did your family start coming to this church?" she asked. When Rebecca said that they had been attending for about six months, Paula asked, "Are your parents comfortable at church? Have they made any good friends yet?"

Rebecca replied that the move had been difficult for her parents. They had been very plugged in at their former church in Houston, and now they missed their friends and church family.

When they arrived at the church parking lot, Rebecca's mother, Shannon, was waiting there to pick up her daughter. Paula got out of the car and introduced herself, and the two women visited for about fifteen minutes. In the course of conversation, Shannon expressed how difficult it was to start all over again in a new community. She was longing to feel at home, she said.

After exchanging phone numbers, Paula invited Shannon's family to sit near hers in church the next morning so she could introduce them to some other church members. Later Paula called Shannon and suggested that they sit together at an upcoming women's ministry luncheon. She also put the couple in touch with some of her friends in various church ministries so Shannon and her husband could find an area of service to plug in to.

We all need to be open to enlarging our circle of friends. If you have ever moved to a new area, you know how much it means to have someone include you in an already established friendship network. Making friends really comes down to applying the Golden Rule: Do unto others as you would have them do unto you. That's what Paula did when she reached out in love and friendship to Shannon.

Growing Deeper with Good Friends

As a good friendship blossoms from an acquaintance-level relationship, new opportunities arise for fun and fellowship. Here are several creative ideas to help you enjoy your good friends.

Picnic in the Park

If it's that pretty-weather time of the year, meet your friend at a nearby park and have a picnic. Split the responsibilities for food, or stop by a local restaurant for takeout. If kids are in tow, picnic near a playground so they can play while you and your friend enjoy the fresh air and sunshine.

Recipe Exchange

In our part of the country, *Southern Living* is a very popular magazine. It's chocked full of decorating and food ideas. The recipes are fantastic, and they are much more fun when tried out with a friend. When you find a recipe you want to try, invite a friend over to cook it with you or simply to test the results. Perhaps she has a new recipe she wants to try, too, and you can cook and taste together.

Sale Watch

Call your friend when you notice a great sale at one of her favorite stores, or keep an eye out for a deal on something you know she likes.

Terry Ann reflects: One of my friends knew I had been looking for some time for a certain style of bedspread. When she was out shopping, she happened to see one that she thought I might like. It had all the right colors; but more importantly, it was a deal! A quick phone call and several hours later, I'd made a dynamite purchase—and shared an enjoyable bargain-hunting moment with a friend.

❋ ❋ ❋

Garage-Sale Rendezvous

If you have the ability to see the "gem in the junk," find a friend with the same keen eye and set aside Friday or Saturday mornings to hit garage sales and yard boutiques together. If you happen to find an entire neighborhood having its annual garage sale, you've hit a gold mine! Remember to go early. If the sale starts at 8:00 A.M., plan to arrive at 7:45, hot coffee in hand, and be the first ones to dash into those garages laden with potential treasures. Keep a list of what other friends are looking for so you can make the purchase for them if you see the right item.

Best-Restaurant Hunt

Once a month, get together with a few friends and scout together for the best restaurant in your area. Decide what the criteria will be for judging a restaurant and then pick a new place to visit for lunch each month. In the Dallas–Fort Worth metroplex, we have restaurants galore, so we don't have much trouble finding new ones. If you live in a small town, you may want to visit nearby towns once a month or rate a different entrée each month at a popular restaurant.

Local-Program Watch

Make plans to go to a special program together—say, a lecture or seminar by a famous author or speaker, a school band concert, or a local football game. These and other events such as church programs, fashion shows, and community meetings are being scheduled continuously in most cities. Keep an eye out for a special event, call up a friend, and enjoy it together.

Christmas Cheer

Yes, the holidays are a busy time; so as you enjoy some of the festive spirit of the season, enjoy it with someone. Invite a friend to go with you to the annual Christmas pageant, festival, or bazaar. It will be a memory in the making! Go ahead and buy an extra ticket or two, knowing that you'll find someone who will go with you.

Java Enjoyment

Meet at the local coffee house on a regular basis (for example, the first Tuesday of every month) for a "sip and share." Use this time to visit with one another and share at least one joy and one grief. As friends we need to be available to "rejoice with those who rejoice, and mourn with those who mourn" (Romans 12:15).

Kids' Stuff

Sometimes the interests and activities of kids draw moms together. We can build friendships on them! Consider meeting another mother at the school after you both drop off your kids and go out for breakfast together. Or plan on driving to the soccer game in the same car. Take the kids to paint pottery, while the two of you visit and/or paint too. Go to the zoo or museum; they're both wonderful places to bond with friends while the kids have fun and learn something new.

Friendship Workout

Get together with one or more of your friends and enjoy exercising together. We know of a group of women who walk every Monday, Wednesday, and Friday after dropping off their children at school.

They park their cars and vigorously walk and talk for about an hour. They get a good, consistent cardiovascular workout and enjoy each other's company at the same time.

A Movie and Dessert

Be on the lookout for new movies coming to the local theater that might interest you and a friend. Plan on going out for dessert after the movie so you can have some time to discuss the movie, laugh, and share about life.

Birthday Celebration

Remembering someone's birthday can be a significant step in building a friendship. Join together with several friends to begin a birthday dinner club. The birthday girl chooses the restaurant, and the others bring funny cards and maybe flowers. This tradition can carry on for many years. Why not take a few minutes today and mark your friends' birthdays on a calendar at home or work? Then visit a card shop and buy cards for all of them at one time. Organize the cards, stamps, and addresses in one convenient place near the calendar. That way, if you can't attend the birthday luncheon or dinner celebration, you can at least send your card in a timely fashion.

Charitable Companions

Choose a charity that you and your friend can serve in together—for example, feeding the homeless, sorting clothes for a clothes drive, or volunteering at a hospital. As you serve together, you bless others as well as your own friendship.

We know of a group of women who organize an Easter celebration every year for children who have been removed from their homes because of abuse. These children are being cared for by the state while they wait for placement in foster homes. The women involve their own children as they conduct an Easter egg hunt, provide wonderful food, and give away candy, toys, and Easter baskets filled with goodies. More importantly, they share the Easter story and tell the children that the Lord loves them and has a wonderful plan for their lives. What a great way for friends to work together for the good of those who are less fortunate! And what a great opportunity for these women's children to see the importance of joining hearts and hands to bless others!

Home-Interior Makeover

This is one of our favorite ideas. Don't you have a friend whose home always looks so inviting? She has a knack for creating a beautiful environment. She has the ability to choose colors, fabrics, carpet, paint, and decorator items and then put them together in such a way that her house looks like something out of *Better Homes and Gardens*. How does she do it? Well, why not invite her over for a great lunch in return for her decorating advice? If she has children, offer to baby-sit for her a few times in exchange for her creative tips. Give her complete freedom to make suggestions. You may find that a simple rearrangement of your existing furniture and knickknacks gives your living room a whole new look. Or perhaps a new, exciting paint color (one you never would have considered in a million years) would be just the thing to spiff up the bedroom without costing an arm and a leg. Just think what a compliment it will be to your decorator friend when you ask her advice on how to make your little corner of the world more eye appealing!

Friendship Luncheon

Once a year invite several of your good friends over for a luncheon.

There is a time for everything, and a season for every activity under heaven….a time to weep and a time to laugh, a time to mourn and a time to dance. —Ecclesiastes 3:1, 4

91

Break out your finest dinnerware and prettiest tablecloth. Cook the meal yourself, or have each person bring either an appetizer, salad, main course, or dessert. Use place cards at the table to indicate where each person should sit. This will give the ladies who don't know each other well an opportunity to make a new friend or two. Invite someone who is new to your church or neighborhood so they can meet your group of friends. What a great way to honor your friends and start a tradition that you can keep for years to come!

Memorable Moments for Soul Mates

Often times we take our special "friends of the heart" for granted. We know they will always be there for us, and we know they love us unconditionally, so we may not think to plan for quality time together. But soul mate friendships are so unique and valuable that we really ought to put time and effort into nurturing them and enjoying them. Certainly, the activities listed in the preceding section are good things to do with our closest and dearest friends. But here are several additional ideas reserved specifically for soul mates.

Weekend Retreat   Charlston ~ Savana - April - May

Choose a date for a "Girls Weekend Away." Then pick a nearby town to visit and reserve a hotel room, or get a room in a bed-and-breakfast or a quaint country inn. If you live in a small rural town, perhaps the fun thing to do would be to visit the closest big city. Plan activities around your common interests, whether that's shopping or museums or movies. Bring the photographs you've been taking all year long and spend time scrapbooking. Do some research ahead of time to identify some great restaurants. You may want to plan some discussion topics for your trip, including those things you want to think about and pray through together. Consider making this an annual event!

Goal-Oriented Get-Together

Choose a half-day to get together with a soul mate and talk about the directions your lives and careers are taking. Bounce ideas off of each other and deliberate over issues that need work. Pray and plan, remembering that, as Proverbs 27:17 tells us, "iron sharpens iron." Be there for each other and hold each other accountable to your goals. Cap off your time together with dessert or a meal, and enjoy the depth of fellowship that comes from building your lives together.

After-the-Storm Regrouping

When life brings a difficulty or even a tragedy, it is often healing to spend some time with our closest friends to work through the anxiety or grief. When you've faced a particularly hard struggle, plan a time alone with one or more of your soul mates to pray and work through the challenge together.

Purposeful Play Day

Plan at least one day a year that you will join with one of your soul mates to do something new, fun, and creative. It may be learning a new hobby together at a local craft store. It may be going to an exercise or cooking class together. Go ahead. Give it a try, and have a blast!

Phone-a-Friend

Many times our soul mates don't live close by. Airfare is expensive, and visiting one another even once a year can be difficult. That's when there's nothing better than a long, relaxed, old-fashioned, heart-to-heart gab session via the telephone. Consider establishing a once a month phone marathon with your friend. Schedule it on the calendar, just like you would a doctor's appointment or a conference with your child's teacher. Take turns initiating the call so you can split the long distance costs.

Following Jesus

When we choose to make friends a priority and enjoy doing things with them, we are imitating none other than our Lord and Savior, Jesus. Even a cursory look at his life shows that he spent many enjoyable hours talking and eating with people. We know from Scripture that he attended weddings, ate dinner with new acquaintances, and even stayed in some of their homes. Clearly, he enjoyed sharing downtime and relaxing in the presence of his good friends, and he shared both laughter and joy with those few who became his soul mates.

Let's laugh and have fun with our friends too. Let's share the joys and the griefs of our lives with them. And as we do, let's rest in the knowledge that we're right in the center of the will of God for our lives, because we're following in the footsteps of Jesus.

POWER POINT

⚙ **Read:** Luke 10:25–42. Here we have two stories about relationships. Name the people in these stories who were not open to love and relationships. Then name the people who seemed to value relationships and who showed it by their actions. With whom do you best relate?

✎ **Pray:** Most loving heavenly Father, I praise you and thank you for the joy of friendship. Thank you for the great joy I've found in my friendship with you. Thank you also for the joy that comes from

94

spending time with good friends. Please bless the time I share with these friends. Help us to grow to enjoy each other more and more as we laugh together and weep together. May we continuously rejoice together in you. In Jesus' name I pray, amen.

💡 **Remember:** "A cheerful heart is good medicine" (Proverbs 17:22).

☺ **Do:** Take a moment right now to call one of your friends—either someone you know quite well, or someone with whom you have a new and budding friendship. Make a plan to enjoy time together using one of the ideas in this chapter, or come up with an idea of your own. Whatever you decide, as the commercial says, "Just do it!"

Power Principle #3

THe P🌸wer oF giving

We make a living by what we get, but we make a life by what we give.

—Winston Churchill

Give, and it will be given to you. A good measure, pressed down, shaken together and running over, will be poured into your lap.

—Luke 6:38

Generating Generosity
The Gift of Talents, Time, and Treasure

We can give without loving, but we cannot love without giving.

—Author unknown

Patti is a giver. However, on the surface, many may mistakenly think she is a taker. Nothing could be further from the truth. From her wheelchair Patti gives love, kind words of encouragement, prayers, and blessings to all that know her. The physical effects of multiple sclerosis have not taken away from her ability to significantly impact others by giving herself to her friends. The fortunate volunteers who visit Patti's home each week to help during the day while her husband teaches school are enriched by their association with her, all agree.

One volunteer named Leslie relates that during her visits, Patti always asks about Leslie's family, activities, and life. And on nights when Patti has difficulty sleeping, she lies awake in bed and prays for the lives and families of the people who visited her that day.

Patti gives in ways that most of us don't even remember to give. She gives an ear willing to listen, a smile willing to encourage, and a heart willing to care. Patti is a beautiful example of one who gives despite physical handicaps, chronic pain, and possible excuses. She is a happy and whole person because of her attitude toward life and toward other people. Yes, Patti's friends have served her and given to her in significant ways in order to help her through her debilitating illness; but all of them will tell you that they are the ones who have been given a gift.

Giving comes in all different shapes, sizes, and venues. Some people give time or talent. Others give resources. A listening ear, a warm embrace, even a home-cooked meal are all things we can give to build bridges to others. We learn from Patti's example that each of us can be givers in some form or fashion, and we shouldn't allow life circumstances to provide excuses for us.

Essentially, giving is the act of thinking about how to meet a need in someone's life and then doing it. It is love in action—putting feet to the kind thoughts and feelings we have toward someone. It's the eruption of thoughtfulness toward another person. It's also a key building block of positive friendships.

What Can You Do for Your Friend?

To borrow and twist a phrase from the late President John F. Kennedy, "Ask not what your friends can do for you, but rather what you can do for your friends." The truth is, we all struggle at times with the desire to get for ourselves. We want to give; we know we need to give; but honestly, deep down inside, we also want to receive. Chalk it up to our innate selfishness. (Come on, admit it. There's a little bit of selfishness in all of us.) But relationships soon fizzle if they are based on the "what can the other person do for me" mentality. We see this in marriages, and we certainly see it in friendships. The challenge for us is to grow to become more of a giver than a taker.

In Luke chapter 6 we find Jesus delivering a discourse to a multitude of people, including his disciples. We know it as the Sermon on the Mount. Here he shares many vital lessons about life, including instructions on relationships and the giving of ourselves to others. In verses 27–36, he encourages us to do the preposterous: to love our enemies and do good to those who hate us. How is this possible? Like gravity, the natural law of "self first" tends to pull at us, making it difficult to climb the challenging mountain of loving and giving to others, even when those people are friends. Yet Jesus continues to lead us up the steep, mountainous terrain with the instruction, "Do not judge, and you will not be judged. Do not condemn, and you will not be condemned. Forgive, and you will be forgiven" (Luke 6:37).

Finally, at the top of the mountain, Jesus plants a flag—the banner of strong relationships: "Give, and it will be given to you. A good measure, pressed down, shaken together and running over, will be poured into your lap. For with the measure you use, it will be measured to you" (Luke 6:38). Perhaps you have heard that very passage quoted during a sermon on giving to meet the annual church budget or building campaign goal. Jesus, however, wasn't talking about material giving. He was talking about being generous with kindness, love, and forgiveness in the context of relationships.

It's easy to condemn, hate, and demand that our needs be met; we do it naturally, in the flesh. These very attitudes, however, alienate us from having meaningful, life-giving relationships with others. We must crawl down from the throne of our own hearts and replace self with the only one who deserves to sit in the place of honor. When we give Jesus Christ his due place in our lives, we become dependent on him to help us forgive, love, and give to others.

Humanly speaking, we can't climb this mountain alone. God's Spirit through us can help us do what doesn't come naturally. As we allow his love to flow through us, God develops selflessness and a beautiful, giving spirit within us, superseding our self-centeredness. We are then able to give in ways that significantly, almost miraculously, bless others.

Recently we heard about a couple who were told by their obstetrician that the baby girl the wife was carrying would not live but a few hours after birth. Friends and family gathered at the hospital to welcome this little one into the world only to then grieve with her parents when her life was over.

Knowing that this heartsick couple was bearing a burden that mere words could not express, an acquaintance from their church, Tracy, gave a gift that could have only been inspired by God himself. While praying for this devastated couple, Tracy had an idea. She made a quick trip to the Christian bookstore, purchased a tiny pink Bible, and had the baby's name engraved on the front in delicate script. The next day she attended the small service at the funeral home and presented the mother with her gift. The heartbroken mother placed the Bible in the wee coffin with that beautiful baby girl.

The funeral service was filled with tears and questions. Why did the Lord allow this precious one to be born, only to be taken away so soon? But it was also filled with faith. At the gravesite, as the mother bent over to kiss her little one for the last time, she slipped the Bible out of the casket and clutched it to her breast. Her tear-stained face was now radiant. She had at least one thing of her daughter's to cherish for years to come: the pink Bible filled with words of God's peace and faithfulness.

On that day, a gift was given for no reason other than to bless the receiver. If we ask the Lord, he will show us how to be gift givers who bless our friends in ways that are divine.

The Joy of Generosity

As we thought about the greatest gifts we've ever received, we concluded that it wasn't the actual gift that was so meaningful, but rather the knowledge that the giver cared for us to the point of wanting to bless us. The fact that someone devoted time, energy, and resources to demonstrate love for us is what makes the gift so valuable.

❖

Terry Ann reflects: This point was driven home to me recently when I received an unexpected gift from two precious little friends.

I have a dear friend named Nancy who is my opposite in many ways. She prefers the quiet of home. I find myself wondering why we pay a mortgage, since I seem to live in the car and only go home to change clothes, pick up one child, and drop off another.

Nancy finds true peace and joy in living an orderly life. I find fulfillment living in a somewhat controlled state of frenzy. You've heard of balancing the checkbook? Well, Nancy actually does it—to the last penny. I, on the other hand, have never balanced my account. Instead, for years I have lived on the faulty premise that as long as there are checks in the check register, there must be money in the account.

Nancy and I do have several things in common, however. First, we both have five children; and second, we both love finding a good deal. We are constantly giving each other fabulous gifts we've found at garage sales. But the sweetest gift I've received in a long time didn't come from Nancy but from her eight-year-old twin boys, Peter and David.

As I was leaving their home one afternoon, the twins came running out to my car, grinning from ear to ear and carrying a piece of yellow, legal-lined paper that was folded up to conceal something inside. I was in a hurry, so I took the paper and its mysterious contents and drove off, vowing to open it soon.

When I reached a stoplight, I unwrapped my gift and discovered a hand-drawn picture of the cross of Christ, three one dollar bills, and the gold top from a cologne bottle. Naturally puzzled and concerned that the boys had given me money, I quickly phoned Nancy. I knew that all five of her sons had been taught to work very hard in order to earn money, and for them to give me three dollars was quite a sacrifice.

"Do you know what the boys just gave me when I left your house?" I asked.

"Yes," came her soft reply. "Isn't it so sweet that my boys wanted to give you a gift?"

I was curious to know what motivated this outpouring of love. Plus I couldn't quite figure out why the boys included the gold bottle top. Nancy explained, "Terry Ann, the boys say that whenever they go to your house, they always make a mess, and you never seem to mind." (They obviously had no idea how much I sinfully fretted over the clutter produced from daily living.) "They just wanted to give you a gift to say thank you for all the times you've let them come to your home to play."

She continued, "They wanted to give you something valuable; and knowing that gold is very costly, they wanted you to have the gold top from their daddy's cologne bottle. They know that money is valuable, so they gave that too. And of course their love for God motivated them to draw the picture of the cross."

I have saved that special gift and have often reflected upon it. What touches me about it is not the actual gift but rather the boys' desire to demonstrate their love and appreciation for me in the greatest, most sacrificial way they knew how.

❀   ❀   ❀

Some people are consummate gift givers. They spend months looking for the perfect Christmas, birthday, or graduation gifts for friends and family. Whatever they give is always perfect. They devote much time, thought, and creativity to demonstrating their love through the art of gift giving.

That's what God did when he sent and then sacrificed the greatest gift of all. The giving of his Son, Jesus Christ, was not a quick, flippant afterthought. From the beginning of time, our heavenly Father knew that we would need a gift that would not only fill the void in our hearts, but also pave the way for an eternal relationship with him.

When Jesus gave us life through his death on the cross, the only thing on his mind was us. True giving, the kind that deeply blesses others, happens only as we put the needs of others first. When we spend time with God, he opens our eyes to supernaturally see the needs of others. Then he nudges us to be his heart and his hands to meet those needs.

Giving Your Talents

All of us, at certain times in our lives, feel as if our well has run dry. We believe that we have nothing significant to give to others. At such times, it's critical that we consider what God has to say about us. In Romans 12:6–8 we find these words:

> We have different gifts, according to the grace given us. If a man's gift is prophesying, let him use it in proportion to his faith. If it is serving, let him serve; if it is teaching, let him teach; if it is encouraging, let him encourage; if it is contributing to the needs of others, let him give generously; if it is leadership, let him govern diligently; if it is showing mercy, let him do it cheerfully.

This passage makes it clear that God has equipped each of us for good works. He has given each of us gifts and talents, and he expects us to use them. When we think of the word *talent,* images of world-class skaters, pianists, vocalists, and painters come to mind. But talents are not limited to the world of great artists, musicians, and athletes. God has uniquely gifted us all. He grants us special talents and abilities because he wants us to use these giftings to bless others.

Take a minute to make a list of your natural, God-given abilities and interests. What are some of the things you do well? Maybe you easily recognize the good in others, and you find it quite natural to praise and encourage the efforts of those around you. If that's you, then you need to look for opportunities to applaud loudly when your friends do something well. Cheering a job well done is a wonderful gift to give! Maybe you have a natural tendency toward organization, and you would enjoy organizing a friendship reunion or neighborhood social. Then plan away, tending to every detail, and bless your friends with a wonderful event. Or volunteer to help a frazzled and harried girlfriend to organize her laundry room, closet, kitchen, or garage.

Janet blesses her friends by taking her camera to almost every event. All year long she takes pictures of her friends' children in various activities, develops the film, and then sticks the photographs in the mail. What a nice surprise to find, tucked in with a mailbox full of bills, a card from Janet that includes pictures of your smiling children! She uses her photography skill as a means to give wonderful gifts to her friends.

Charla has the incredible gift of being able to take a rather mundane-looking room and, with little or no money, turn it into a room to be admired, full of warmth and charm. Simply by rearranging the furniture, painting the walls a different color, and placing decorator items in eye appealing groupings, Charla is able to create a living space to be envied by all. The good news is Charla doesn't limit her talent to her own home. She enjoys seeing the potential in the homes of her decorator-deficient friends. She would never insult a girlfriend by giving uninvited "tips."

But when asked for her opinion, she not only makes a suggestion, she offers to lend a hand in transforming the ordinary into the spectacular.

Susan is a gifted gardener. Her quaint, picturesque home surrounded by English-style country gardens exudes a sense of serenity and simpler times. She knows a lot about plants and landscaping and is happy to share her gardening knack with those she holds dear. How blessed are Susan's friends when they drive up to their own homes and enjoy the beauty of her landscaping help! Because Susan is willing to go to the nursery to give advice on what to purchase, and because she is willing to get dirt under her fingernails to design the garden and do the dirty work that landscaping requires, her friends receive an invaluable gift!

Diane possesses the gift of wisdom. Not only does she have much knowledge about what God's Word has to say on many different life issues, she has the God-given ability to take that knowledge and apply it to everyday life situations. Diane uses her gift of wisdom to encourage her friends to make wise choices. She does not force her gift on those who are blessed by her friendship, but rather makes herself available to give counsel when called upon.

We all need to take inventory of our God-given talents and abilities. If we have trouble identifying our gifts, we can ask our family and close friends what they see in us. These are gifts given to us from God. They are not to be hoarded or hidden; they're to be given away to others.

Giving Your Time

Karol reflects: As I was working on this chapter, an unexpected knock came at the door. It was a young friend who needed some advice and a shoulder to cry on. Her counseling session was not on my list of things to do that day. But she needed the gift of an attentive ear and loving care, so I chose to step aside from "my stuff" for a while to offer that gift. Later that day another friend called who simply needed to talk about some issues in her life. Both of these women needed me to give them my most precious commodity: time.

❖ ❖ ❖

Certainly there are occasions when we must guard our time, and in the next chapter we will address boundaries we can set for ourselves. But sometimes the best gift we can give someone is time, even if it's not convenient or easy.

❖

Terry Ann reflects: Recently I was on the receiving end of the wonderful gift of time. It was the holiday season, and Jay and I were hosting a party that really required much of my personal attention. But I was on a tight deadline to finish an all-consuming work-related project, and I literally didn't have the time I needed to get our house in order for the event.

Out of the blue, my friend Karen called with news of an incredible gift. "Terry Ann, I want to give you an early Christmas present," she said. "I have a housekeeper, and I thought it might bless you if the day before your party I sent her to your home instead of mine. Could you use her services?"

What a question! Years ago I would not have accepted. But I am getting much better about being a receiver, so I promptly and gleefully replied, "Yes, yes, yes! And thank you, thank you, thank you!"

Then my friend Jill called and said, "Terry Ann, I know you have a heavy load right now, so may I make, stamp, and mail your party invitations?" Once again my newfound receiving ability kicked in, and I happily agreed. Both friends gave a gift of treasure (Karen paid the housekeeper and Jill paid the postage). But even better, they gave me what I needed most: the gift of time.

❀ ❀ ❀

Time is a precious gift we can give to our friends. But if we are tightly scheduled to the hilt, we leave little room for flexibility, and the opportunity to give our time can pass us by. Granted, the solution may not be to leave empty spaces in our schedules so we can twiddle our thumbs and be ready when someone calls; but we can make a conscious decision to grant the gift of time to our friends and loved ones.

In fact, the two aspects of giving time that are essential to building positive friendship are *staying flexible* and *planning deliberately*. Let's examine how both can help us in giving the gift of time.

Staying Flexible (Having Margins) ā husband friends-

Sometimes we have things on our calendars that we are not able to shift, such as certain meetings, engagements, or deadlines. But other things can be adjusted. Flexibility requires discernment to recognize what can wait and what is nonnegotiable. An open attitude, which releases the need to control every moment, is essential.

Some women struggle with this more than others. There are those who set their schedule for the day, and they are determined to stick to it no matter what. Others allow themselves to be continuously distracted by interruptions and never get anything done. Certainly there is a healthy balance. The important thing is to not get fixated on our own personal agendas to the point that we aren't willing to give time to meet needs in the lives of our friends.

How do we find a healthy balance when it comes to being flexible? Here are some questions to ask yourself when you see a friend in need.

- Is this an immediate need, or can it wait?

- If I change what I have on my schedule in order to meet my friend's need, who will be adversely effected?

- How vital is the activity I had planned to do during this time?

As we mentioned earlier, flexibility is a matter of attitude. Dogged determination is important in many aspects in life, but if it leaves others continually reeling in its wake, we may need to rethink our determination. In this race of life, is the goal to get to the finish line first? Or is it to help as many others as possible cross the finish line with us?

We're reminded of a story we heard about a Special Olympics competition in Seattle, Washington. In one particular race, nine special contestants lined up at the mark. The gun went off, and they started down the track at their meager pace. They'd not gotten far when one of the contestants tripped and fell, crying out as he hit the ground.

One by one the other runners stopped, turned around, and went to the aid of their fallen friend. A girl with Down syndrome kissed his boo-boo, while another said, "It will be alright." Then, in a gesture of perfect love, the contestants joined arms and walked across the finish line together. The crowd began to cheer and continued for several minutes, realizing the beauty of the life lesson they had just observed. For you see, winning is not all about getting there first. It's about stopping along the way to help others experience victory too.

Planning Deliberately

Sometimes a need arises, and we must respond spontaneously. But sometimes we can plan to give our time to others.

Meredith is a business executive who is on the board of directors for several nonprofit organizations. She is very wise in a number of areas, and numerous individuals seek her counsel. Some of these are friends, while others are just acquaintances. With such a full schedule, Meredith found herself feeling frustrated because she often couldn't stop long enough to meet with those people she really wanted to help.

That's when she decided to set aside every Friday to meet with these individuals over lunch. Her plan to set this time aside in her weekly schedule not only solved her problem, it also provided an opportunity to move individuals who were in her circle of acquaintances into her circle of friends. Several vital and meaningful friendships have blossomed through this deliberate plan to meet together.

Discernment is important when it comes to how to best use and plan our time. There are certain friends we know we would never see or keep up with if we didn't set aside an intentional, regular time to meet together. So let's do it! Right now, take a moment to think of someone you would like to develop and maintain a close relationship with. What about that woman who, if you spent any time together at all, you feel sure would click with you and become a great friend? Pick up the phone, or the next time you run into her, schedule a time to meet for lunch. Positive, quality friendships require planned, quality time.

Giving Your Treasure

Who doesn't like to receive a present? The fact that someone thinks of us and then actually goes to the trouble of picking out a special something for us is flattering and honoring. Creative gift giving is an art—an art that we should all develop, because it adds such a fun dimension to all our friendships. It gives us one more way to say, "I care."

In his book *The Five Love Languages,* Dr. Gary Chapman explains that people primarily express their love and care for one another in one of five basic ways. One of the five is the giving and receiving of gifts. He concludes, after having studied cultural patterns around the world, that gift giving is a fundamental expression of the way people feel about one another. Yet visual symbols of love—such as gifts that can be held in your hands—are more important to some people than to others, he says.[1]

If you have a friend who is constantly giving gifts to those around her, you can bet the art of gift giving is highly important to her. You can also safely conclude that when she receives a gift, she hears the loud and clear translation, "I am appreciated and loved."

Whether or not gift giving is our number one love language, we can all agree that to give or receive the gift of "treasure" is pure pleasure! The problem for many of us is not that we don't want to give creative and timely gifts to our friends; it's that we're so busy with life that we don't take the time to do so. Or maybe we simply don't remember that a birthday or anniversary is approaching. Here are a few suggestions to make the joy and art of gift giving a more manageable mission for all of us.

Birthday or Anniversary Calendar

Take an hour to make a list of special friends, and then call each one to get their birthday and anniversary dates. (If you don't already have their addresses, get those too.) Record their names, special dates, and addresses on a special calendar, and hang the calendar where you will see it daily. At the beginning of each month, look to see who you need to purchase a card or gift for, and then do it. Go ahead and address and stamp the card, then simply wait until the appropriate day to mail it.

Gift Closet

Creating and filling a gift closet is an especially great idea if you are Betsy Bargain Hunter. Always be on the lookout for potential gift items that have been reduced 50 to 75 percent. Specialty stores that carry decorator items, candles, stationery, and scented hand lotions almost always have an area in the back where they display their sale items. Garage sales can also provide a gold mine of potential gifts. Stash your great finds in a designated place in your home or office. Not only will you save money on gifts in the long run, but in many cases you will be able to give a nicer gift (monetarily speaking) than if you're forced to buy something on the spur of the moment. And the next time you find yourself wishing that you could give a hurting friend a gift of encouragement, but you haven't got the time to shop—not to worry! A well-stocked gift closet is just the answer.

Gift Certificates

Gift certificates make giving easy. Who wouldn't enjoy a gift certificate for a manicure, pedicure, or massage? Gift certificates for restaurants, book stores, and coffee bars are also nice. Why not combine a gift certificate with a card stating that you will accompany your friend on the outing to redeem it? That way you also get to enjoy one another's company.

Coupon Book

Create a personal coupon book and fill it with coupons redeemable for such things as a free house-cleaning or a night of baby-sitting so your friend can have a date with her husband.

Anonymous Financial Gift

Unexpected medical bills, a corporate layoff, or even a divorce can leave those we love in difficult financial straits. What a joy it can be to pay a light bill, make a house payment, or simply deliver an envelope of cash to a needy friend! Unfortunately, we're not often in a position to help others with monetary needs, because we choose to live lifestyles that don't leave us with much left over. Be prayerful about how you spend the money the Lord has granted to you. Be willing to listen to him and then obey his instructions if he directs you to meet a financial need in a friend's life. Do it anonymously, since people often feel funny or awkward about receiving a financial gift. You may be surprised at the greater joy that comes when you give an anonymous gift, knowing that you will receive nothing in return.

Sacrificial Giving

Karol reflects: Several months ago I received that one letter in the mail that no one particularly jumps for joy to receive: the infamous jury summons. These letters never come at a convenient time! I was summoned to serve just as Terry Ann and I were trying to put the finishing touches on this book. But God's plans and purposes for us go far beyond what we can think or imagine.

During my personal devotional time on the morning of my jury duty, I came to Psalm 37:5: "Commit thy way unto the LORD; trust also in him; and he shall bring it to pass" (KJV). I knelt and prayed, "Oh Lord, order my steps this morning. I commit this jury duty day to you. And if possible, could you allow me not to be called for service?" I rose from my prayer knowing that God would lead me just where I needed to go.

As I entered the giant jury room in downtown Dallas, I had one objective on my mind: find an electrical outlet so I could plug in my computer and work while I was waiting. I walked the perimeter of the room, which was bulging with people, in search of a single little outlet. Finally I saw it. It was in the back, and—glory be!—there was an empty seat near it on the back row. As I sat down, I noticed that the older African-American man sitting next to me had the Book of Psalms in his hand. I struck up a conversation and immediately knew that this man was a gift from God. His name was Bobby Roberson, and he had been walking closely with the Lord for many years. He spoke of his love for the Lord with a deep-rooted confidence, joy, and peace. We talked the entire morning about the many ways God had worked in each of our lives.

Bobby told me a story that happened to him many years ago when he first moved to Dallas. He was making forty dollars a week, and his rent was ten dollars a week. It was a meager income, considering that he had to support his wife (who was going to nursing school at the time) and two kids. It was during this time that Bobby became aware of one of his neighbors in need. She was a woman with three young children and another one on the way. Her husband had left her, and she didn't have the money to pay rent for a place to live. The compassion of Christ rose up in Bobby's heart; and even though he didn't have much himself, he paid her ten-dollars-a-week rent along with his own for several months.

"I couldn't leave her without shelter," Bobby told me. "She needed help. I knew I had to give."

Was it a sacrifice for Bobby and his family to give? Absolutely! Yet Bobby chose to meet the need anyway. He was like the good Samaritan we read about in the Power Point in chapter 6. And Bobby continues to live a life of giving, keeping his eyes open to see the needs of others.

"When I empty out and give to others, I receive," he said. Looking at him, I knew it was true. He was the picture of a man who had received joy and blessing from God. He was one of the most gracious and giving people I have ever met, and he never stopped talking about his love and faith in God. The joy of the Lord is most certainly his strength.

Bobby and I come from two different worlds, but our hearts were able to connect through our mutual love for the Lord. Bobby

It is more blessed to give than to receive. —Acts 20:35

☺

taught me about giving in a new and fresh way. He reminded me that giving is not about giving from our excess, but giving from our hearts. Sometimes giving requires sacrifice. Sometimes it's not easy. But it's always worth it.

I believe my encounter with Bobby was divinely arranged. Bobby helped me see the beauty and joy of sacrificial giving lived out in action. He gave me something that day, although he probably didn't even realize it: He gave me a living testimony of the blessings of giving and an inspiration to live it out in my own life.

❖   ❖   ❖

Willing to Receive

For some of us, being a giver has never been the problem. We spell our middle names G-I-V-E! Where our struggle lies is in being a good receiver. Perhaps it's a pride problem. We don't want to let anyone know that we have a need. We pride ourselves on being self-sufficient, almost to the point of taking insult if friends try to lighten our load by giving us their time, talent, or treasure. Our silent thoughts scream, *Don't they know I can handle it? Do they really think I am so weak and needy?*

Or maybe pride isn't the problem. Maybe we're not good at receiving because we think we're not worthy of receiving. We feel we don't deserve, for whatever reason, being helped or ministered to. The tragedy of this mindset is that not only do we miss out on tremendous blessing, but we rob our friends of the joy that giving brings.

There is a difference between selfishly taking and graciously receiving. Yes, it is more blessed to give than to receive. But receiving has its time and place too. Positive friends are those who willingly, cheerfully give and humbly receive gifts from one another, knowing that whatever gift is given—whether of time, or talent, or treasure—it is an expression of a loving and caring heart.

POWER POINT

⚙ **Read:** 1 Kings 17:7–24 and Mark 12:41–44. Here we have the stories of two giving widows. What do you learn about sacrificial giving from these passages? How were both of these women showing obedience to God in their giving? Notice that it wasn't the size of the gift, but the willingness to give it, that was important.

♡ **Pray:** Glorious and giving Lord, you are the ultimate giver. Thank you for giving me life. Thank you for giving me gifts and talents. Thank you most of all for giving me salvation through your Son, Jesus. I am truly grateful for the work you have done in and through me. Continue to pour your love through me to my friends and family. Open my eyes to opportunities to give to the people you have placed in my life. Help me to know how and when to offer help and encouragement to those in need. Show me how to give love in all its different forms. You are the one I look to for guidance, strength, and help to give to others. In Jesus' name I pray, amen.

💡 **Remember:** "Give, and it will be given to you. A good measure, pressed down, shaken together and running over, will be poured into your lap. For with the measure you use, it will be measured to you" (Luke 6:38).

☺ **Do:** Is there someone in your life who needs a gift? It may be the gift of an encouraging note, a phone call, or a meal. It may simply be the gift of time. Determine today how you will give to someone else. Write a reminder note to yourself and place it where you will see it daily. The note can read something like this: "Whose day have I brightened today?"

Blessed Boundaries
A Gift to Yourself

Having clear boundaries is essential to a healthy, balanced lifestyle.
—Drs. H. Cloud and J. Townsend

By nature most women are people pleasers. We tend to be nurturers who want to fix situations and make everything right. Unfortunately, we get ourselves into trouble when we try to be all things to all people. How we need to realize that just because we *can* doesn't mean we *should!* Just because we're *asked* doesn't mean we should *accept*. The truth is, if we really care about others, sometimes the word *no* must be uttered. Unfortunately, many of us are taught early in life that in order to get along, in order to succeed, in order to serve, in order to be accepted, we must be perpetual doers, continually nodding "yes, I can" and smiling "yes, I will," until we no longer know who we are and why we do what we do.

Both of us are challenged when it comes to boundaries, because we both love people. We are compassionate, and sometimes this can get us into sticky situations. It's hard to know when to draw the line.

❧

Terry Ann reflects: I'll never forget the morning the call came in. It was around 9:45 A.M., and my cohost and I were going off the air in

119

fifteen minutes. I worked for "the best country in the city"—102.5 FM KJNE, a radio station based in central Texas. "Jane" was my on-air name, and I represented half of the morning duo, Jane and Jay. I never minded rising at 4:00 A.M. Monday through Saturday in order to be prepared and on the air by 6:00 A.M., because I loved my work.

We had just come out of a music set with a public service announcement about drug addiction, when the engineer put a call through to me from a listener named Wilma. Wilma cried as she told me that she was worried about her two grandchildren, who were both under the age of two. Apparently her son and daughter-in-law were putting the little guys to sleep at night by blowing marijuana in their faces. Wilma had heard the public service announcement about drug abuse, and not knowing where else to turn, she was now pleading to me for help.

My on-air partner finished up our show so I could talk at greater length with our troubled listener. I found myself asking Wilma if I could come to her house to share what I felt sure would be the answer to her problem.

The next day I found myself sitting in a run-down house in a neighborhood I wouldn't catch myself dead in after dark, listening as Wilma's life story unfolded. Here was a hurting woman who had been divorced four times and had lived much of her life as a prostitute. She had a prison record and a long history of drug and alcohol abuse. She had little money and no hope.

God use me, I pleaded silently. I wanted so much to be a tool he could use to heal a life.

Sharing my heart with Wilma meant sharing my Lord. I knew he was the only one who could make her new. He was the only one who could take her broken and scarred life and restore peace, joy, and purpose. She bowed her head, and with tears streaming from her pain-filled eyes, she earnestly prayed to receive Christ as her Savior.

Afterward I asked sincerely, "What are your needs, Wilma?" It was a simple question. But I was surprised by her answer.

"Could you please pay my electric bill, because the service is about to be terminated?"

I felt great joy as I blessed her in this monetary way. After all, my dollars weren't actually mine. I was simply responsible to spend the money God had entrusted to me in a way that pleased him. I knew that the giving of my finances was an act of worship to my Savior.

But it wasn't long before I became Wilma's money tree. One month, it was the electric bill. The next month, the electric bill *and* the phone bill. Day after day, week after week, bill after bill, I helped out until it finally hit me: I was not helping at all. Robbing Wilma of the fulfillment that comes from learning to do things God's way (getting a job is biblical!), I was causing her to place her dependence on me rather than teaching her to apply the instruction found in God's Word.

As much as we would love to believe we can be all things to all people, the truth is, we cannot, and we should not! It was time for me to tell my new friend no. It was time to recognize that my part in helping was over. My help—which she mistakenly viewed as her never-ending cash supply—had become her crutch.

To this day I wonder if Wilma just used me to get her bills paid, all the while thinking how easy it was to take me for a ride. I would like to believe that she truly felt she needed me and had sincerely asked for help with an attitude of gratitude. But, truth be known, it doesn't matter. Either way, I had crossed over the boundary line from help to hindrance.

❧ ❧ ❧

Perhaps you're thinking, "Terry Ann, that woman took you to the cleaners! What a sucker you are!" But hold on. Paying someone's bills for an extended period of time while she sits around doing nothing may be an extreme example, but most of us allow people to take advantage of us in other ways. Maybe you allow a friend to continually monopolize your time as you listen hour after hour to her complain about life in general. Or maybe you're the one who is always called upon to change your plans in order to accommodate a friend's schedule. At times we all overextend ourselves in order to heed someone else's request or demand.

It's a wonderful thing to be kind, compassionate, and flexible. But being a pushover time and time again helps no one. It only enables others to be selfish and inconsiderate.

What we need to do is learn to accept only those tasks that come from the hand of God. After all, he is the only one whose opinion of us ultimately matters! We must surrender our desire to be man-pleasers in order to become God-pleasers. The key is learning when and how to say the word "no," because if we say "yes" to every request and "OK" to every opportunity that comes our way, we will wind up exhausted, frazzled, resentful, and discouraged.

Developing Discernment

Creating appropriate boundaries in our lives requires wise discernment. To discern means to judge closely or examine carefully—and that's exactly what we need to do when it comes to meeting the needs of others. On the one hand we want to be loving, kind, and open to everyone. On the other hand we have limitations, and we can't do everything. Discernment is essential for knowing when, where, and how we are to give to others; it guides us in recognizing true needs.

Solomon said, "How wonderful to be wise, to be able to analyze and interpret things. Wisdom lights up a person's face, softening its hardness....Those who are wise will find a time and a way to do what is right. Yes, there is a time and a way for everything, even as people's troubles lie heavily upon them" (Ecclesiastes 8:1, 5–6 NLT).

We all know women who seem to have an uncanny discernment about people and situations. They're the ones who say, "I can't put my finger on why, but something doesn't feel quite right." Later you find out something *wasn't* quite right. Perhaps you are one of these discerning types. Many of us, though, struggle to have insight. The good news is that discernment can be sought and found if we look for it in the right places. Proverbs 2:2–6 says,

> Make your ear attentive to wisdom,
> Incline your heart to understanding;
> For if you cry for discernment,
> Lift your voice for understanding;
> If you seek her as silver
> And search for her as for hidden treasures;
> Then you will discern the fear of the LORD
> And discover the knowledge of God.
> For the LORD gives wisdom;
> From His mouth come knowledge and understanding. (NASB)

God is our source for discernment and wisdom. He is the one who gives us eyes to see and hearts to understand the needs around us. That's why our search for discernment must begin on our knees in prayer: "Lord show me, direct me. Is this what I should be doing with my time? Does this person really need to talk, or does she just want to grumble and complain? Is this a need that you have called me to meet

I cannot do everything, but still I can do something; and because I cannot do everything, I will not refuse to do something I can do. —Edward Everett Hale

in this person's life? Is this the place I am to serve? What do you have for me to do at this moment?"

As we reverently lay our requests before God, he is faithful to direct our paths. Proverbs 3:5–6 reminds us, "Trust in the LORD with all your heart and lean not on your own understanding; in all your ways acknowledge him, and he will make your paths straight." This must be our banner verse as we consider what we should and should not do with our time and resources. We can't allow feelings, emotions, or guilt to direct our paths—only God.

Watch Out for Takers

Throughout our journey on earth we will encounter people with a wide variety of needs, perspectives, and approaches to life. Some, for example, will be givers, while others will tend to be takers. When we enter into a relationship with a taker, we need to exercise wisdom, because such people often have no respect or concern for our time and needs. Our Christian instinct to love, serve, and give can be hijacked, and we can find ourselves held captive to a relentless, self-absorbed, smooth-talking, time-monopolizing, guilt-supplying, innocent-looking-but-very-needy taker. If we don't use discernment, this person can entice us to do and be anything and everything but what God has called us to do and be.

You probably don't have to think long to remember a time when someone took advantage of you. Maybe a coworker allowed you to do most of the work on a big project but didn't hesitate to share equally in the credit. Maybe a mother at your child's school manipulated and maneuvered teachers, coaches, and other parents to arrange a situation to benefit her children—to the detriment of yours and everyone else's.

Sometimes the ones taking advantage of us are women we call our "friends." When that's the case, we often do the easy thing and just go along with them. *Why rock the boat?* we think. And at times, going along to get along may be our best option. We have to learn to pick our battles. But some takers will push our limits to the point that we have to say, "You know, enough is enough."

Of course, not every person who asks us for a favor or requests that we serve in a particular area at church, school, or work is trying to take advantage of us. But just because someone asks doesn't mean we should accept!

Yes, God does call us to give, but he doesn't call us to give out. He calls us to serve, but not to be sucked dry. He calls us to water others, but not to the point that we wither. We need to learn to do two important tasks simultaneously: giving and guarding. We need to learn to give openly and freely to others while guarding ourselves from committing to people and things that God has not called us to. Discernment is necessary for both.

Yes or No?

When someone requests something of us, how do we know whether to say yes or no? Four questions can help us discern what to do:

1. Will it really help this person? Meeting every need and responding to every whim of the people around us is neither love nor service. In fact, sometimes the most loving thing we can do is to say no and let them learn from the natural consequences of their actions.

Mothers in particular have trouble applying this principle. Take Karen for example. She lovingly (and mistakenly) knocks herself out for her four children by attempting to cater to their every request and "need." When her youngest continually forgets to put his lunch in his backpack and goes to school lunchless again, never fear—Mom to the rescue! Her second trip to school that morning not only ensures that little Johnny has lunch, it also ensures that he will continue to forget it!

When we say yes to everything, when we try to meet every perceived need, we take away the responsibilities of others, and that's not true love or help. We actually do a disservice to the ones we care about.

2. Have I sought God's direction? Jesus didn't cater to whims or selfish requests. In Matthew 12:38, the Pharisees and religious teachers asked Jesus to show them a miraculous sign to prove that he was from God. (They had obviously ignored the numerous signs he had already performed.) We may think that Jesus should have gone ahead and performed another miracle right then and there. After all, what would it hurt—especially if it would make all those religious leaders believe?

But Jesus discerned that even if he did present a show of miracles in front of the crowd, they would not be satisfied. He had already healed the sick, given sight to the blind, raised the dead, and changed water into wine. They had all the proof they needed. No, although Jesus could have done what they asked, he did not. He knew he had not been put on this earth to cater to people's whims. He had come to do the will of the Father. He wasn't sent to be a crowd pleaser or to prove himself to others; he came to please and serve his Father and his Father alone.

Of course, doing his Father's will at times required him to perform miracles, even in front of crowds—but only at the direction of the one who sent him! Isn't that freeing? As believers in Christ, we have not been chosen to be God's beloved in order to please and serve a husband, a child, a parent, an employer, or a friend. We have been chosen to cater to the desires of the Father. This means we are to serve others under his direction and by his instruction. He will call us to serve our family and friends in his way and his time.

3. What is my motive for helping? Why do you want to help this person? Is it out of love? A sense of obligation? The fear of rejection? When our need for approval and acceptance leads us to say yes when we shouldn't, we quickly find ourselves in over our heads, doing things God never intended for us to be doing. This tendency to be people pleasers can literally run us ragged—and we have no one to blame but ourselves. We are most definitely called to love others by giving and serving. But we are not called to give to all people and serve all people at all times.

4. Is this what I'm supposed to do right now? In Matthew 12, as Jesus was teaching the crowd, someone told him that his mother and brothers were asking to speak to him. Surely Jesus could stop what he was doing, at least for a minute, to go out and see them. After all, they were family!

But Jesus didn't do the expected thing. He used his family's request as a teaching opportunity, saying, "Who is my mother, and who are my brothers?" Then, pointing to his disciples, he said, "Here are my mother and my brothers. For whoever does the will of my Father in heaven is my brother and sister and mother" (Matthew 12:48–50).

Scripture never tells us if Jesus went to talk with his family. What we know for sure is that he didn't drop everything in order to immediately run to them. Instead, he continued with what he was doing, with what God had called him to do at that moment—teach the people—before he turned to other things. Obviously, he knew the situation and the needs better than we do. Through his God-given discernment, he knew when to do what his family was asking and when not to.

Beautiful Boundaries

What do good boundaries look like? Clearly what's right for one person may be wrong for another. A pastor's wife is likely to have different defined boundaries in her life than, say, the office manager of a small business.

Take Barbara and Becky, for example. They are two women with two different sets of boundaries. Barbara, who is married to a minister, rarely takes a phone call from a friend after 6 P.M. Because her husband is often called away from the house to minister to people at odd hours of the night, she protects the window of time between six and bedtime in order to have quality time with her husband. Becky, on the other hand, is an office manager, and she has no time during her workday for even a quick chat with a girlfriend. But her husband works the late shift, so the time between getting home from work and bedtime is her own, and it often includes calls to her friends. She wouldn't dream of gabbing away the weekend on the phone, however, because that's her only opportunity to spend quality time with her husband.

Of course, setting boundaries, especially with friends and family members, isn't easy. In fact, it may be one of the hardest things we are called to do within the context of friendship. It's only when we understand that boundaries are established because we love others and want the best for all concerned that we find the strength, courage, and fortitude to establish them. Boundaries are not brick walls meant to keep people out of our lives; they're simply helpful guidelines to guard us from squandering our time, talents, and treasure on the selfish demands and whims of others.

Often boundaries don't need to be established until we see a need for them in a certain area or with a certain person. Let's say, for example, that you begin a friendship with Lisa. You enjoy chatting with her on the phone, but soon you begin to realize that she is a complainer who gossips about the other ladies in your church group. Her daily calls are beginning to monopolize your time and fill your mind with negative thoughts toward others. *Aha!* A boundary becomes a necessity.

How do you set an effective boundary? By following these five steps:

1. Realize

When you make the realization that you need a boundary, you have taken the first step in the right direction. Often we let things go on for too long and allow ourselves to become completely exasperated before we do anything. Be alert! When someone or something begins to encroach on your life to the extent that you're being diverted from the path you need to follow, then it's time to set a boundary.

2. Pray

Once you realize there's a problem, take it to the Lord in prayer. Ask God for his guidance and direction in handling the situation. James 1:5 reminds us, "If any of you lacks wisdom, he should ask God, who gives generously to all without finding fault, and it will be given to him." Our loving, giving heavenly Father is ready and willing to impart the wisdom you need to make a prudent decision. Ask the Lord to either cause the situation to resolve itself or create an opportunity for you to talk about the boundary in love. Then ask him to give you the courage, boldness, and obedience to follow through when the opportunity you prayed for arises.

3. Speak

Declare the boundary. For example, say, "Lisa, I value your friendship, but I can't spend a lot of time chatting on the phone. I have several projects that I really have to get done." You may even feel compelled to add, "I must tell you that I'm uncomfortable with talking about other people behind their backs, so when you call, I would like to keep our conversation on a positive note." Speaking the truth is not always easy, but when it's done in love, it's always right. The Word of God tells us, "The truth will set you

FRee!

free" (John 8:32). When truth is spoken with the proper motivation—with a heart intent on righteousness and love—the hearer will ultimately receive a blessing, even if it comes in the form of correction.

4. Remind

Don't assume that just because you've expressed a boundary, it will automatically be observed. In fact, you can almost expect a new boundary line to be crossed for two reasons: the other person will forget, or he or she will want to test it to see if you were really serious. A point will come when you will need to gently remind the encroacher that the boundary is still in place. You will have to say something like, "Lisa, I need to remind you that I don't feel comfortable listening to stories about other people. I'm sure you mean no harm, but I'm serious about this. I value our friendship so much that I must insist that our conversations stay positive."

You might add, "And don't forget, I'm under several deadlines, so I have to keep our conversations to a minimum. I'm truly looking forward to spending more time with you when my load lightens up. Thank you for understanding."

5. Enforce

The toughest part of setting a boundary is enforcing it. But not enforcing the boundary will only lead to further anger and frustration. The next time the phone rings and it's Lisa, you may need to enforce the boundary by not taking her call. Wow, that's a tough one, and hopefully it won't come to that! But some people are stubborn; they refuse to take the hint and change. Or they're so engrossed in their own wants and needs that they have no respect for anyone else's.

Enforcing a boundary is like disciplining our children: It's the hardest part of the process for us, but it's also the part that helps the other person the most. If we allow others to live their lives with no consequences, they will never learn. We actually help boundary-encroachers to become better people by expecting them to live responsibly. Boundaries are necessary for our protection and for their good.

Trusting God to Fill in the Gaps

Karol reflects: When my friend Nancy went through a terribly dark and difficult period in her life, I wasn't there for her. There were many reasons why I couldn't help her at that time, one of the most prominent being that I had just had my second daughter. With two children under the age of two, my hands were full and my energy was spent. I was barely able to run my own household, much less reach out to others.

But several years later, when my mother was tragically killed, Nancy reached out to me, offering both comfort and help. I confessed to her how awful I felt about not having helped her during her dark days. She encouraged me to let go of the guilt immediately, and then she said something profound: "You know, Karol, God always provides the people we need in our lives at the time that we need them."

God provides! During Nancy's struggle, God brought certain people who were the perfect ones to surround her and her husband at that time. She was buoyed up in God's comfort and love through the people he sent.

We can't be there to meet every need of every individual in our lives. Only God can do that. And he will!

When a need arises, our first responsibility is to look to the Lord for direction. To what extent does he want to use us to fill this gap or meet this need? We must go only where God calls us and equips us to go—and then trust him to fill in the gaps. He is the Great Provider, not us! He may choose to use us, and then again he may not. If we insist on being someone's need-meeter when God has not called us to the task, the person God *has* chosen to fill the gap doesn't get to do his or her part.

The important thing is to listen for God's call. This is not an excuse to be lazy or selfish; it's a call to be wise, discerning, and obedient. We need to be women who have hearts and minds filled with discernment, always ready to follow God's direction, rather than women who jump to our own loud inner voices of guilt, obligation, and rejection.

Let's take a look at Psalm 34:4–10 as a reminder of how wonderfully the Lord provides for each of us:

> I sought the LORD, and he answered me;
>> he delivered me from all my fears.
> Those who look to him are radiant;
>> their faces are never covered with shame.
> This poor man called, and the LORD heard him;
>> he saved him out of all his troubles.
> The angel of the LORD encamps around those who fear him,
>> and he delivers them.
>
> Taste and see that the LORD is good;
>> blessed is the man who takes refuge in him.
> Fear the LORD, you his saints,
>> for those who fear him lack nothing.
> The lions may grow weak and hungry,
>> but those who seek the LORD lack no good thing.

God may very well use you to meet someone's need by calling you to offer comfort, help, or support. Or he may use someone else if you are not able. Just remember: The greatest thing we can do for our friends is point them to the one who can truly meet their deepest needs. He is their healer, their provider, and their strength in times of trouble. If we will exercise discernment, obey God's voice, and point people to the Savior, we will be positive friends indeed.

POWER POINT

⚙ **Read:** Ephesians 4. What does this passage teach you about boundaries? Why do you think Paul included verse 28? What guidelines for communicating with others do you find in verses 29–32?

♡ **Pray:** Wonderful Lord, thank you for the example Christ set in his life on earth, showing us how to give freely while also establishing healthy boundaries. Please grant me discernment and wisdom in dealing with the people in my life. Allow me to recognize when boundaries are necessary. Help me to establish wise guidelines and to enforce them in love and kindness. Open my eyes to see the true needs of others, and show me what part you have for me in meeting those needs. Thank you that you are the Great Provider. I trust you to always fill in all the gaps. In Jesus' name, amen.

♀ **Remember:** "Be imitators of God, therefore, as dearly loved children and live a life of love, just as Christ loved us and gave himself up for us as a fragrant offering and sacrifice to God" (Ephesians 5:1–2).

☺ **Do:** Are there any encroachers in your life right now? Do you need to set some boundaries? Prayerfully walk through the steps in this chapter and verbalize your guidelines to the person(s) this week.

Are you currently encroaching upon someone else's boundary? Take a candid look at your relationships and consider your own neediness in relation to others. What changes do you need to make in order to be less demanding? Read Psalm 34 out loud whenever you need a reminder that God is your Great Provider. Taste and see that the Lord is good!

Power Principle #4

THe P wer of l yalty

A true friend…advises justly, assists readily, adventures boldly, takes all patiently, defends courageously, and continues a friend unchangeably.

—William Penn

He who is true to one friend thus proves himself worthy of many.

—Anonymous

9

The Friendship Price Tag
Sacrifice and Trust—a Must

To be capable of steady friendship and lasting love are the two greatest proofs, not only of goodness of heart, but of strength of mind.

—William Hazlitt

It must have been summer. It was hot, the lawns were green, and children were out playing. Abbey remembers the day as if it were yesterday:

She was eight years old, and the neighborhood kids were gathered at a home one street over from Abbey's house. Brenda, her best friend, was crying. A line had been drawn with chalk across the driveway, and all the kids were on one side of the line. All, that is, except Brenda. A self-appointed "queen" had loudly pronounced that no one wanted to play with Brenda. A challenge was issued: If anyone crossed the line to play with Brenda, they too would be ridiculed and deemed a second-class citizen—for that day anyway.

Abbey's heart was beating fast as she looked at the line, which seemed as big as a chasm cutting through a mountain range. Brenda was her friend, her best friend! And she had done nothing wrong. Her crime was nothing more than having been randomly picked to be the social outcast for that day.

Abbey knew that crossing the line meant risking her reputation. The "popular" kids would view her in the same negative light as they now viewed Brenda. But as Abbey saw the tears slowly stream from her best friend's big brown eyes, she knew what she must do.

Abbey looked in the stone faces of the rest of the children then took the plunge. That one step across the baby blue chalk line turned out to be a monumental leap of friendship. Hugging her dear friend in solidarity did at least as much for Abbey as it did for Brenda. The sense in Abbey's heart that she had done the right thing by sticking by her friend felt so good!

Sacrificial Friendship

Loyalty is a rare find today. It can cost a great deal. But a loyal friend is beyond worth.

Loyalty is a virtue that depends heavily on the existence of at least two other virtues. Read how *The American Heritage Dictionary* defines the word *loyal:* "Steadfast in allegiance; faithful to a person, ideal, or custom." A quick look around us tells us that steadfastness and faithfulness are in short supply these days. Our society as a whole has been programmed to look out for number one; or, as someone once put it, "grab all you can, can all you get, and then sit on the can." Steadfastness, faithfulness, and loyalty tend to fall by the wayside as soon as they require the sacrifice of personal gain or comfort.

American culture has not always been this way. As products of parents who married in the 1950s and raised us in the '60s and '70s, we witnessed the change in the American work culture as company loyalty toward its employees began to vanish. When we were young girls, it was commonplace to see a friend's grandfather retire from his job having given thirty, forty, or even fifty years of service to one company. For the most part, those days are long gone—not only in the workplace, but in so many areas of life.

Consider modern-day couples. All of us probably know at least one woman who seems to live in constant fear that if she doesn't continue to "measure up"—if she doesn't get her face injected with botoxin, her lips plumped, her brows waxed, her breasts lifted, her tummy tucked, and her thighs suctioned—then her husband may just trade in her forty-year-old body for two twenties. And we don't mean twenty-dollar bills!

Expediency is the name of the game. People are loyal to others as long as they still make them look good, feel good, or put money in their pockets. Unfortunately, when people are in relationships only for what they can get from them, the environment becomes devoid of trust. Welcome to our world!

Who then can we trust? As Christians we know that the only one worthy of our complete trust is our heavenly Father, who loves us in spite of our shortcomings. At the same time, we have a need to feel safe in relationships with other people. For the sake of our emotional well-being, we have a need to connect with positive and loyal friends.

The Beginning of a Beautiful Friendship

In 1 Samuel we see a beautiful picture of a friendship built on loyalty. The loyalty that David and Jonathan shared is evidenced in the sacrificial love and unwavering trust between them. Their story is one of our favorites in the entire Bible.

❀

Terry Ann reflects: A few years ago, I directed a children's musical by Kathie Hill, *Famous Kids of the Bible,* that set the friendship of Jonathan and David to words and music. In order to help the second through fourth graders understand the deep commitment these friends

Jonathan had David reaffirm his oath out of love for him, because he loved him as he loved himself.
—1 Samuel 20:17

vowed to one another, I illustrated the plot with a modern-day twist.

"Boys and girls," I told them, "I want you to close your eyes and imagine with me that your dad is the ruler of the city. He is the King Tut of the Dallas–Ft. Worth metroplex. He owns it all—the government, the zoo, Six Flags over Texas, and all the water parks and swimming pools. He owns the Dallas Cowboys, the Texas Rangers, the Dallas Mavericks, even the Dallas Stars hockey team. Not only that, he owns everyone's house and apartment. He has more money, power, and fame than anyone. And guess what? Because you are his son or daughter, when he dies, it will all be yours! You will be the richest person in the world one day.

"Now imagine this. Your father comes to you and says, 'I've made a decision. Even though you have been a wonderful child, I've decided that when I die, you will not be the next king. You will not be in charge of my estate. I am going to leave it all to your best friend.'

"Wow! Can you imagine your dad leaving everything that should have been yours to your best friend? How would you respond? What would your attitude be? Would you be happy for your friend? Would that person still *be* your friend?"

❀ ❀ ❀

That's not exactly what happened to Jonathan and David, but it's close. First Samuel 17 begins their story by telling us that David, an Israelite, was the youngest of eight sons. He stayed home to tend the family sheep while his three oldest brothers followed King Saul into war against the Philistines. The ancient Greeks, to whom the Philistines were apparently related, sometimes decided battles by having the two sides choose champions to meet in one-on-one combat. They believed that through this economy of soldiers, the judgment of

140

the gods could be determined on whatever matter was at stake.

God is so amazing! He lovingly orchestrates circumstances for us in such a way that his purposes are served, and we are blessed. We see this principle at work in the lives of David and Jonathan. In 1 Samuel 17:4–5, 8–11 we read:

> A champion named Goliath, who was from Gath, came out of the Philistine camp. He was over nine feet tall. He had a bronze helmet on his head and wore a coat of scale armor of bronze weighing five thousand shekels....Goliath stood and shouted to the ranks of Israel,..."Choose a man and have him come down to me. If he is able to fight and kill me, we will become your subjects; but if I overcome him and kill him, you will become our subjects and serve us." Then the Philistine said, "This day I defy the ranks of Israel! Give me a man and let us fight each other." On hearing the Philistine's words, Saul and all the Israelites were dismayed and terrified.

Around this time David was sent by his father, Jesse, to take food to his older brothers, who were on the front lines of the battle. David was thrilled with this prospect.

He already had the reputation of bravery. Sometime before he'd been summoned to King Saul's court to sooth the king's troubled soul with his beautiful harp playing. One of Saul's servants had described David to the king this way: "I have seen a son of Jesse of Bethlehem who knows how to play the harp. He is a brave man and a warrior. He speaks well and is a fine-looking man. And the LORD is with him" (1 Samuel 16:18).

David probably met Jonathan, Saul's son, for the first time when he came to play the harp for the king. We don't read about their friendship at this point. But David's music did turn out to be just what Saul needed, and he quickly found favor in the king's eyes.

When David arrived at the battlefield with the food for his brothers, he saw Goliath step out from the Philistine line and shout his usual threats. Looking around, he noticed that the Israelite soldiers were quaking with fear over the prospect of having to fight the giant. He began questioning the soldiers about the reward that would go to the man who brought Goliath down.

David's brothers were enraged, because they knew what he was thinking. *Here we go again,* they thought. *Our cocky little brother thinks he's so tough!* But word got back to King Saul that there was an Israelite in the ranks who was willing to challenge Goliath. Well, you know the rest of the story. David, by the power of God, killed Goliath. He was then brought before King Saul while still holding the giant's head.

This is the scene where we see the roots of loyal friendship take hold in Jonathan's heart. In 1 Samuel 18:1 we read that "after David had finished talking with Saul, Jonathan became one in spirit with David, and he loved him as himself." David had probably explained to King Saul that his battlefield actions were an expression of his obedience and love toward a faithful God. Upon hearing this, Jonathan decided then and there that David was the kind of person he wanted as a friend. His friendship with David was built upon the foundation of mutual reverence, love, and obedience toward God, their heavenly Father.

A Test of Loyalty

But here is the amazing thing—the "God-thing," if you will. Because Jonathan, like David, walked with God, he probably had a sense that David would be a great leader in the kingdom one day. He even may have known, somewhere deep in his spirit, that David, not he, would be the next king of Israel.

The hand of God was clearly upon Jonathan's best friend. David was becoming a household name. First Samuel 18:5 says, "Whatever Saul sent him to do, David did it so successfully that Saul gave him a high rank in the army. This pleased all the people, and Saul's officers as well." Women started dancing in the streets, singing, "Saul has slain his thousands, and David his tens of thousands" (v. 7).

What a test of friendship was brewing! What a test of loyalty was in the making! Jonathan's best friend—just like the best friend in the little made-up story for the children's choir—was about to have it all. King Saul's torch of power and riches was going to be passed not to his son, Jonathan, but to David.

For most of us, that would be a hard pill to swallow. Jealousy and revenge would be our middle names. Unless we were truly abiding in God's presence and strength, we'd be hard-pressed to handle ourselves with love and dignity—best friend or no best friend.

So here's the question. How loyal are you? If your friendship with someone were to begin to cost you something of value—say, money, time, or reputation—would you remain faithful? Anything of value always comes with a high price tag! Are you willing to pay the costly price of loyalty in your relationships? Are the friends you have chosen worth the price that loyalty might require?

When Jesus chose *us* as friends, it cost him everything. It cost him his life. He loved us and valued our friendship so much that he paid the ultimate price in order to have us live forever with him. He was faithful to the point of death. Most likely we will not be asked to die a physical death for our friends. But when the price gets high, will we be faithful?

Choosing Your Friends Wisely

Positive friends are loyal friends. They're people we can trust. And we all want to be surrounded by people we trust, don't we? If you are a business owner, you want to trust your employees. If you are a mother who works outside the home, you want to trust your childcare provider. Parents want to trust that their children are safe with teachers at school and church. Homeowners want to trust that when the air-conditioning repair man says they need a new compressor, that's really the case. And we all want to trust the mechanic who fixes our cars. Even more, we want to trust the people who are closest to us—our spouses, our parents, our children, and our friends.

Trust is built on two key ingredients: honesty and dependability. As children we start out trusting everyone and anyone. We begin our life's journey wanting to believe that no one would purposely do us harm. All too soon, however, we realize that trust is something we must grant to others only as they consistently display honesty and dependability. Trust is something that cannot be conferred or bought, only earned.

We've both had the privilege of being raised in families in which trust was never violated by our parents or siblings. Our parents have been faithful to each other for decades, and our sisters (neither of us has a brother!) have truly rejoiced in our successes and cried with us in our sorrows over the years. This safe home environment led us to freely extend trust to friends and acquaintances as we entered into the teenage and college years and then into early adulthood. However, in both our lives, our easy willingness to trust has caused us to be burned in relationships on several occasions. We've learned to forgive and move on, but we've also learned the importance of choosing friends we can trust.

When Trust Is Violated

Women who've have had their trust severely violated by someone they care about find it extremely difficult to feel secure in future relationships. Maybe you know such a woman. You've been on the verge of a good friendship with her for a long period of time, but you can't seem to go any deeper. You can do little more than scratch the emotional surface. Of course, it may be that you have less in common with this woman than you think. It may be that she doesn't feel a need to pursue another meaningful friendship. Or it may be that she has serious trust issues. She may have been deeply wounded by her parents or peers during her growing-up years, and now she has difficulty trusting a new friend.

As we travel and speak to women around the country, we never cease to be amazed at how many women have emotional scars because someone they loved and trusted sold them out in some way. Once their hearts have been broken, they feel as if they have nothing left to give to others. And who can blame them for not wanting to go through what they have already experienced? Pain and rejection aren't feelings most of us want to repeat! To avoid them, many women construct great iron walls around their hearts. They fortify those walls with suspicion and doubt and a firm resolve to never be hurt again.

Maybe this is where you are living. You are determined that you can make it on your own. You don't need anybody. It's just you and God. No one else will ever get close enough to hurt you again. Oh, hear us! We all bring baggage from our pasts into our present relationships. But God didn't create us for a life of emotional solitude. God created us in his image. He made us like himself—as relational beings. God created Adam and desired fellowship with him. But he knew that Adam needed more. He knew that Adam needed emotional intimacy with another human being.

We are no different. We need people in our lives. People who really know us. People we can trust. When our trust is violated—and it will be, because people and relationships are never perfect—we must learn

how to forgive, pick ourselves back up, and trust our loving heavenly Father to bring other people into our lives who can help restore and refresh us.

We're not saying we should be gluttons for punishment. Consider the story of the ten-year-old boy who walked six blocks to school every morning. Day after day, as he rounded one particular corner, he was met by a group of boys who said they wanted to be his friends then knocked him down and took his lunch money. It wasn't long before this boy realized he needed to take a different route to school!

For our emotional well-being, we have to strike a balance between entering friendships with casual, blind trust on the one hand and viewing every person we encounter with wary regard on the other. Trust isn't something we just hand over to anyone. Neither is it something we hold so tightly that we never allow anyone to get close to us. We simply must be wise in choosing who will have the high privilege of being our close friends.

How Do You Choose?

Why is it that girls, upon entering the fourth grade, seem to disappear into the "catty zone" and don't reappear until they're about seventeen? When our daughters were this age, they began coming home with stories about different little girls in their classes who were mad at each other one day and best friends the next. They would say things like, "Cathy isn't friends with Lauren anymore, and Hailey's new best friend is Robin."

We used these stories as opportunities to teach our girls what true friendship is all about. We both told our daughters, "If you hear a girl speaking badly about another girl behind her back, you can count on that same girl talking behind your back too." We explained that by

146

observing the behavior of their classmates over time, they would be able to choose friends who would prove faithful.

Choosing friends is not something we should do in a haphazard way. Jonathan observed David and saw that he had a heart for God. He observed David's loyalty toward his father, King Saul. His observations led him to the conclusion that David would be a loyal and trustworthy friend—a wonderful friend of the heart.

Teaching our daughters at early ages the value of observing people in order to choose friends wisely is a lesson that should serve them well throughout life. Many times, catty little girls grow into catty women. They have never learned to be secure in who God has made them to be. Therefore, even as grown women—and yes, even grown women in the church—they are still trying to make themselves look better (in their own eyes at least) by belittling others.

If you are missing the emotional closeness that true friendship brings, ask the Lord to bring the right friends into your life. Carefully observe the women in your neighborhood, office, school, or church before choosing whom you want to be close to. Remember, you do have a choice! Then as the Lord, in his timing, deepens these special relationships, be willing to be open to your friends and trust them with your heart.

When Your Life Is on the Line

Let's say a coworker was competing with you for a promotion, but she was still willing to come to you privately after discovering an error in your work so you could correct it before your supervisor discovered your mistake. Wouldn't you feel that you could trust her? Would you trust the employee at the dry cleaners who found a ten-dollar bill in your shirt pocket and returned it to you? Would you trust someone who put his or her own life in danger in order to save yours? In all three scenarios someone was willing to place your need above their own need or gain. Someone was willing to sacrifice self-interest for your best interest.

Friendship often requires the kind of sacrifice that promotes trust. We know that Jonathan was required to sacrifice great personal gain on behalf of his friend David. David, meanwhile, was required to make his own sacrifice: He had to let go of past baggage that might cause him to be distrustful and place his complete trust in Jonathan. This was no easy task for David.

David knew that Jonathan loved him. Jonathan had even made a covenant with him as a sign and seal of their friendship. In the covenant ceremony recorded in 1 Samuel 18:1–4, Jonathan took off his royal robe and gave it to David, along with his tunic, his sword, his bow, and his belt. But in the weeks and months that followed, David had plenty of reason to wonder how far Jonathan could be trusted. When push came to shove, could he trust his friend with his life?

After David's defeat of the giant, Goliath, King Saul had decided to keep David on in his court. But his admiration for David quickly turned to hatred as he realized that David's popularity in Israel was beginning to eclipse his own. You would think that Saul would have been thrilled to have a mighty and loyal warrior like David working on his behalf. By the power of God, David was leading the Israelite army into victory after victory. But because King Saul no longer had his eyes on the Lord, he was concerned about his own reputation. He wanted the praise and approval of the people all to himself. He had become a people pleaser, seeking the applause of others at every turn, instead of desiring the approval of God—the one who had enabled him to be king in the first place.

Isn't this what we often do? Take our eyes off of God and his purposes and turn them to our own self-interest? Isn't this the reason we see so much gossiping and backstabbing going on between woman and girls? When we have our eyes on ourselves instead of the Lord, we are concerned about protecting our popularity, our "power base." But when our eyes are focused on the Lord, we are free to love others and rejoice with them in their successes. We are able to trust a loving heavenly Father to be the lifter of our heads (see Psalm 3:3) and seek his approval above all else.

David was able to have unwavering trust in Jonathan—he could be certain Jonathan would never sell him out, even to King Saul—because he knew that Jonathan's eyes were on the Lord. Jonathan was loyal above all to God and his purposes. That enabled him to put aside personal gain in order to further God's will for his best friend, David, and all the people of Israel.

God Is Our Refuge

Later in the story of Jonathan and David, King Saul set a trap for David, fully intending to kill him. Jonathan found it difficult to believe that his father would take the life of his best friend. Because he wanted to trust his father, he defended him to David. But David replied in 1 Samuel 20:3, "Your father knows very well that I have found favor in your eyes, and he has said to himself, 'Jonathan must not know this or he will be grieved.' Yet as surely as the LORD lives and as you live, there is only a step between me and death."

Jonathan then took a courageous step. He told David, "Whatever you want me to do, I'll do for you" (v. 4). He set out to discern for certain the motivations of his father's heart toward David. When he discovered that David's life was in fact in jeopardy, he helped David escape King Saul's wrath.

David took refuge in a cave; but more importantly, he took refuge in Jonathan's friendship. Jonathan knew David's hiding place, but he never betrayed him. David felt safe, knowing he could trust his best friend.

When we have trust, we feel safe. And don't we all need to feel safe? Even David, whose acts of bravery were known far and wide, needed that feeling of security.

But as much as we would like to (and sometimes do) put our total trust in people, we know that people aren't perfect. They fail. Even our closest friends will disappoint us at one time or another. But God's Word tells us "there is a friend who sticks closer than a brother" (Proverbs 18:24).

God himself is our refuge. We can run to him and forever feel safe. He will never fail us! His friendship toward us is sacrificial; it cost him the life of his only Son. He can be trusted because he is honest, and what he says about us in his Word is true. He is dependable; he is always there for us and will never leave us. Certainly, we want to seek out loyal friends here on earth and be loyal friends to others. But we must always remember that God is the ultimate Loyal Friend. Let's keep our eyes on him.

POWER POINT

⚙ **Read:** Matthew 26:14–16, 47–50. Why do you think Judas betrayed Jesus? How did Jesus respond to his disloyalty? How do you think Jesus felt about the betrayal after having had Judas serve with him for three years? Now read Matthew 27:1–10. How did Judas feel about his own disloyalty?

☝ **Pray:** Faithful Father, how good it is to know that you are my safe place! I can always put my trust in you and find refuge in your unfailing love. I praise you for your loving-kindness! Help me to be faithful, both to you and to others. Help me to find loyal friends like Jonathan and David, and give me the courage and conviction to stand by them through good times and bad. Thank you that you will never leave me. I love you! In Jesus' name I pray, amen.

💡 **Remember:** "A friend loves at all times" (Proverbs 17:17).

☺ **Do:** Take a moment to ponder, pray, and reflect on your friendships. Is there a friend you need to go to and ask for forgiveness because you've been disloyal? Is there a friend you need to forgive because of her disloyalty to you? Instead of allowing your hurt to fester into bitterness and anger, ask God to help you forgive your friend from the heart and move on.

Destructive Forces
Attitudes and Actions That Divide Relationships

Keep well thy tongue and keep thy friends.

—Geoffrey Chaucer

The weather in North Texas is unpredictable, to say the least. We may start out with a warm, sunny day, and by late afternoon, a West Texas storm rolls into town and changes everything. On one particular day in the spring of 2000, motorists drove to work in nice, pleasant weather conditions, but by the time they left for their commute home, they were fleeing the winds of a tornado that struck downtown Fort Worth. Offices were destroyed, homes were demolished, and storefronts were shattered—all in a matter of minutes.

One local news station was able to broadcast the devastation as it occurred using their weather camera, which was perched high atop one of Fort Worth's office buildings. We, the viewers, watched in awe as the rains poured, the winds swirled, and the tornado destroyed. In a very short time the damage was done.

The unbridled power of a storm is a fearful thing! And just as there are natural, destructive forces in the physical realm, there are also natural, destructive forces in the social realm. Unbridled human nature can have as powerful and devastating an effect on relationships as a tornado on a Texas town.

The flooding rains of envy and jealousy, the bitter winds of anger and rage, and the swirling cyclone of gossip can beat upon all of us now and then. These negative forces can uproot friendships; create dissension in families, churches, and neighborhoods; and destroy people's lives in a matter of moments.

In chapter 9 we looked at the qualities that define a loyal friend. We said that loyal friends are faithful, committed, trustworthy, and dependable. But in order to fully understand what something is, sometimes it's valuable to examine what it is not. Therefore, in this chapter, we're going to look at qualities that are diametrically opposed to loyalty. As we do, let's keep in mind that we're not talking about these negative qualities to give us ammunition for judging other people; rather, we're doing a self-check to consider whether or not these qualities exist in our own lives.

Flooding Rains

Suzanne's daughter made the varsity volleyball team; Trisha's daughter didn't. Suzanne was elected to be president of the local PTA; Trisha was overlooked for an office. Then there's the fact that Suzanne lives in a beautiful home, wears designer clothes, and drives a brand new car, while Trisha's family struggles to make ends meet. Suzanne and Trisha have been friends since their daughters started kindergarten together, but envy is beginning to creep into Trisha's heart as she focuses her attention on what Suzanne has and she does not.

Trisha has a choice: She can wallow in envy allowing self-pity, resentment, jealousy, and covetousness to take root and grow. Or she can turn from these destructive thoughts and feelings and replace them with thankfulness and gratitude for the way God is working in both women's lives, each in different ways.

It's so easy to fall into jealousy and envy; it's much harder to turn with love toward contentment and thankfulness! Let's say Trisha takes the easy route. She doesn't check her envy at the door of her heart. Instead, she begins calling Suzanne with only one interest in mind: to find out any negative news that is going on in Suzanne's life.

When she hears that Suzanne is struggling over something with her husband or that one of her children has come home with a bad grade, Trisha feels a little bit better about her own lot in life. Oh, it appears she is calling with the best intentions—to share some school news or just say hello—but once Trisha has gotten a little morsel of negative information, she casually mentions it in conversation to other friends:

"Bless Suzanne's heart, she feels as if she doesn't fit in with the rest of us because she never got a college degree. We need to help her feel accepted." Her comment sounds kind, but it's really a put down!

Or, "Let's pray for Suzanne. She told me she's really struggling with disciplining her kids. Of course, she told me this in confidence, but I'm sure she wouldn't mind if we prayed for her. You know, maybe if she didn't spend so much time going on trips with her husband, she would have more time with her children. Good, strong discipline requires a mother to be at home." How common is that in Christian circles—couching gossip in a "prayer request"?

Or, "I wonder if Suzanne should be serving on the PTA board. She seems so busy, with all the other things she does. Besides, I really question whether she is bold enough to take a stand on the tough issues. Someone should probably talk to the other board members; I'm sure they could find someone to replace her. And it would be a blessing to Suzanne—she needs a break!" Sounds like Trisha really cares, but the truth is, she's making judgment calls that aren't hers to make.

Instead of enjoying a friendship with Suzanne, Trisha has chosen to darken the sky with her clouds of gossip and unkindness. Before long she is no longer able to speak to Suzanne in a gentle way. She probably doesn't realize it, but the slow dripping of envy has turned into the heavy rains of jealousy, flooding her thoughts, actions, and words with a subtle hatred. Not only is the storm destructive to her friendship, but it is destructive to Suzanne's reputation—and to Trisha's.

The Bible speaks quite often about envy and jealousy. Let's take a quick look at several scriptures from both the Old and New Testaments.

- *Job 5:2:* "Resentment kills a fool, and envy slays the simple."

- *Proverbs 14:30:* "A heart at peace gives life to the body, but envy rots the bones."

- *Proverbs 27:4:* "Anger is cruel and fury overwhelming, but who can stand before jealousy?"

- *Romans 13:13–14:* "Let us behave decently, as in the daytime, not in orgies and drunkenness, not in sexual immorality and debauchery, not in dissension and jealousy. Rather, clothe yourselves with the Lord Jesus Christ, and do not think about how to gratify the desires of the sinful nature."

- *1 Corinthians 3:3:* "You are still worldly. For since there is jealousy and quarreling among you, are you not worldly? Are you not acting like mere men?"

- *1 Corinthians 13:4:* "Love is patient, love is kind. It does not envy, it does not boast, it is not proud."

- *James 3:14–16:* "But if you harbor bitter envy and selfish ambition in your hearts, do not boast about it or deny the truth. Such 'wisdom' does not come down from heaven but is earthly, unspiritual, of the devil. For where you have envy and selfish ambition, there you find disorder and every evil practice."

- *1 Peter 2:1:* "Therefore, rid yourselves of all malice and all deceit, hypocrisy, envy, and slander of every kind."

The Bible is clear: As followers of Christ, we must not allow envy and jealousy to whip up a storm in any part of our lives. But how do you stop the deluge from coming? At the first detection of raindrops, take cover under the umbrella of prayer! Begin by asking God to replace your envy with love for the other person. Ask him to replace your coveting with contentment, recognizing that he has a plan for your life as well as for your friend's life—and the two plans are not the same.

Put a guard over you mouth, so that even the tiniest root of envy and jealousy cannot grow into unkindness and slander and gossip. And take refuge in the sure foundation of God's Word by memorizing this passage from Psalms: "Trust in the LORD and do good; dwell in the land and enjoy safe pasture. Delight yourself in the LORD and he will give you the desires of your heart....Be still before the LORD and wait patiently for him; do not fret when men succeed in their ways" (Psalm 37:3–4, 7).

Finally, for all types of weather, put on your "Son-glasses." See the world from an eternal viewpoint and not an earthly one. Realize that God has a bigger picture in mind. As you see a friend succeed, rejoice! Be thankful for the way God is working in your life and the lives of others.

❀

Terry Ann reflects: One of the best things my parents ever taught me was how to rejoice with others when they encountered good fortune. I can still hear their encouraging words when I would run for high school student council or try out for cheerleader: "Remember, Terry Ann, only God can know if the other person needs that victory more than you. Trust him with your life. Know that the way you handle disappointment or defeat says more about your relationship with God than how you handle victory and success."

❀ ❀ ❀

What if you find yourself on the flip side of envying others? Maybe this scenario is familiar: A friend begins to treat you differently for no apparent reason. Her demeanor becomes cold and aloof. She no longer includes you in get-togethers. Phone calls only happen when you initiate them. *What have I done to offend this person?* you wonder. But when you ask, "What's wrong?" she replies, "Nothing," or, "I don't know what you mean."

If this happened to you when you were a child or teenager, and your parents were anything like ours, you probably heard these words: "Don't worry about it. You haven't done anything wrong. She's just jealous." And that was probably the case.

Whether you're on the giving or receiving end of jealousy, go to God in prayer. He alone is faithful. He has a beautiful, eternal plan, and you can trust his unfailing love. Remembering God's faithfulness will help you to desire his best not only for yourself, but for others too. It will dry up the flood rains of envy and jealousy.

Hebrews 12:2 reminds us, "Let us fix our eyes on Jesus, the author and perfecter of our faith, who for the joy set before him endured the cross, scorning its shame, and sat down at the right hand of the throne of God." There are bright days ahead! Put on your Son-glasses, and you'll be prepared to weather life's storms.

Bitter Winds

Lindsey was a little bothered, to say the least, that she wasn't invited to her friend Gloria's dinner party. Granted, the husbands of the couples who were invited were all fishing buddies who had just completed a fishing expedition, and they were getting together to celebrate their big catch. Still Lindsey felt left out. *If Gloria really valued my friendship,* she thought, *she would have asked Fred and me to come, even though Fred doesn't like to fish. And after all, we're friends with the other couples too.*

A few days later, when one of the women who attended the party had the audacity to bring pictures of the fish fry to their Wednesday morning Bible study, Lindsey didn't know whether to be hurt, angry, or both. *Gloria doesn't have to be so excited about seeing the pictures,* she fumed. *It's as if she's parading the party in my face.*

Several weeks later Lindsey decided to have a little dinner party of her own. Guess who wasn't on the guest list? What started out as a light breeze of bitterness had grown into the full-blown winds of anger and revenge. Lindsey was determined to outdo the fish fry and put on a dinner party to be remembered. She sent out cute invitations far in advance to many of Gloria's friends, hoping the cards would be seen on their refrigerators for weeks. And of course, the Wednesday after the party, Lindsey brought pictures to show at Bible study.

But Gloria didn't react the way Lindsey expected her to. *She's just pretending that she doesn't care about not being invited,* Lindsey thought, nearly exploding with rage. The truth of the matter was that Gloria was quite unaware of Lindsey's bitterness and anger. She had no idea that Lindsey had been hurt over the fish fry. She also felt secure in her friendship with Lindsey, so the fact that she and her husband weren't asked to Lindsey's get-together didn't faze her.

Oblivious to any problem, Gloria felt right at home when she called Lindsey the next week to see if she could borrow her coffee maker for a shower she was giving for her sister-in-law. That was it! Lindsey's anger was unleashed.

"I can't believe you would call me to borrow something to help you host another party I'm not invited to!" she exploded. "You don't need a coffee maker, you need a friend maker, because you are no

Get rid of all bitterness, rage and anger, brawling and slander, along with every form of malice. Be kind and compassionate to one another, forgiving each other, just as in Christ God forgave you. —Ephesians 4:31–32

friend of mine."

Needless to say, that was the end of Lindsey and Gloria's friendship. It didn't have to end that way. In fact, Gloria is still scratching her head, trying to figure out what went wrong between them. When bitterness first began to blow in Lindsey's heart and mind, she should have dealt with it honestly and directly. Instead she let her bitterness fester and grow until it turned into full-blown anger and rage. If only Lindsey had considered the weather conditions! If only she had told Gloria that her feelings had been hurt over the fish fry!

All of us can find ourselves trapped at times in the wind tunnel of bitterness that leads straight to anger. Whether that bitterness is toward a sibling, a friend, a coworker, or a spouse, we must let it go before it grows stronger.

At the first sign of a bitter breeze, cover yourself (as in the rain storm) with the windbreaker of prayer. Pray, "Lord, help me with these bitter thoughts. Take them away from me and replace them with love and forgiveness, just as you love and forgive me. And show me if I need to go to my friend in love to tell her how I feel."

As the wind continues to blow, be sure to rest securely on the firm foundation of God's Word. First Corinthians 13:5 reminds us that love "is not rude, it is not self-seeking, it is not easily angered, it keeps no record of wrongs." Your love may not be perfect, but God's love through you can be! Our responsibility is laid out clearly in Colossians 3:8: "But now you must rid yourselves of all such things as these: anger, rage, malice, slander, and filthy language from your lips." Paul goes on to say in verses 12 and 13, "Therefore, as God's chosen people, holy and dearly loved, clothe yourselves with compassion, kindness, humility, gentleness and patience. Bear with each other and forgive whatever grievances you may have against one another. Forgive as the Lord forgave you."

Forgiveness and forbearance are the weapons that defeat bitterness. Clothe yourself with these godly qualities.

As with the flood of envy, a key to battling the winds of bitterness is to guard your mouth. It's so easy to let hurtful accusations fly when we're harboring bitterness or resentment. Be careful! "In your anger do not sin," we are told in Ephesians 4:26. Keep your tongue knotted and tied down securely when you know the winds of bitterness are blowing.

And once again, put on your Son-glasses. Exchange the dark glasses of anger with the bright ones of God's love and forgiveness. As you turn your eyes to Jesus, you can't help but see his abundant love and forgiveness toward you. And that makes it so much easier to live out Hebrews 12:14–15: "Make every effort to live in peace with all men and to be holy; without holiness no one will see the Lord. See to it that no one misses the grace of God and that no bitter root grows up to cause trouble and defile many."

The Cyclone of Gossip

The fury of a tornado is quick, powerful, and many times deadly. It's one of the most powerful forces in nature. But as destructive as a cyclone can be in the physical realm, gossip is at least as destructive in the realm of relationships. Both a tornado and the tongue can cause tremendous devastation.

That's why we've mentioned it twice now: Guard your mouth! Not just against angry or jealous words, but against any tendency to gossip about others. In James 3:3–10 we read:

> When we put bits into the mouths of horses to make them obey us, we can turn the whole animal. Or take ships as an example. Although they are so large and are driven by strong winds, they are steered by a very small rudder wherever the pilot

wants to go. Likewise the tongue is a small part of the body, but it makes great boasts. Consider what a great forest is set on fire by a small spark. The tongue also is a fire, a world of evil among the parts of the body. It corrupts the whole person, sets the whole course of his life on fire, and is itself set on fire by hell.

All kinds of animals, birds, reptiles and creatures of the sea are being tamed and have been tamed by man, but no man can tame the tongue. It is a restless evil, full of deadly poison.

With the tongue we praise our Lord and Father, and with it we curse men, who have been made in God's likeness. Out of the same mouth come praise and cursing. My brothers, this should not be.

What makes some people use their tongues for evil, while others use theirs for good? Why are some women given to gossip, while others are given to praise? Typically the cyclone of gossip begins to blow when someone is unwilling to let go of envy, bitterness, or anger, as we've already discussed. But other things can help stir the pot. For example, a woman who is insecure may try to make herself seem important by sharing someone else's news or information. She may not feel she has anything positive to say for herself. At least with gossip, she figures, she's assured of an audience.

Whatever the reason for gossip, there's one thing we can know for sure: If someone talks to us about a mutual friend behind our friend's back, that person won't hesitate to talk about us when *we're* not around. As the saying goes, "Don't talk about yourself; we'll do that after you leave!" We may smile as we read that, but only because we know how close to reality it is.

When it comes to deciding what to say or not say to others, we've found three questions to be helpful: Is it true? Is it kind? Is it necessary? If the answer to any of the three is no, then don't say it!

Darkness versus Son-Light

When we see the raindrops of envy falling, feel the winds of bitterness and anger picking up speed, or sense the potential of a cyclone of gossip, we must recognize the source of these dark storms: our own sinful nature. Scripture points out that the deeds of the sinful nature are in direct conflict with the Spirit of God. And when we're in conflict with God, storms and destruction are inevitable! Our only hope for overcoming the darkness of sin is to look to God and allow his Son-light to dispel it.

Ponder the following scriptures and notice the distinction between the dark deeds of the flesh and the light of God's truth:

> Furthermore, since they did not think it worthwhile to retain the knowledge of God, he gave them over to a depraved mind, to do what ought not to be done. They have become filled with every kind of wickedness, evil, greed and depravity. They are full of envy, murder, strife, deceit and malice. They are gossips, slanderers, God-haters, insolent, arrogant and boastful; they invent ways of doing evil; they disobey their parents; they are senseless, faithless, heartless, ruthless. (Romans 1:28–31)

> The entire law is summed up in a single command: "Love your neighbor as yourself." If you keep on biting and devouring each other, watch out or you will be destroyed by each other. The acts of the sinful nature are obvious: sexual immorality, impurity and debauchery; idolatry and witchcraft; hatred, discord, jealousy, fits of rage, selfish ambition, dissensions, factions and envy; drunkenness, orgies, and the like.…But the fruit of the Spirit is love, joy, peace, patience, kindness, goodness, faithfulness, gentleness and self-control. Against such things there is no law. (Galatians 5:14–15, 19–23)

I don't repeat gossip, so listen carefully! —Anonymous

At one time we too were foolish, disobedient, deceived and enslaved by all kinds of passions and pleasures. We lived in malice and envy, being hated and hating one another. But when the kindness and love of God our Savior appeared, he saved us, not because of righteous things we had done, but because of his mercy. (Titus 3:3–5)

Clearly the deeds of darkness, which are prompted by our sinful natures, are destructive forces in any friendship. But the actions that result from God's Son-light pouring through our lives are relationship strengtheners and builders. We make the choice. Will we allow God's love to pour through us, or will we stifle his love through sin and selfishness?

Making the right choice is easiest at the first sign of bad weather. A full-blown storm of jealousy, anger, and gossip is difficult to turn back, and the damage can be done before we know it. So watch the weather. Be alert to the warning signs for floods, bitter winds, and cyclones, and take the proper precautions. We've talked about these precautions throughout this chapter, but let's summarize them here.

1. Cover yourself in prayer, asking for God's strength and help to love others with his unfailing love.

2. Hide yourself in the firm foundation of God's truth. Fill your mind with Scripture and those things that are true, noble, right, pure, lovely, and admirable (Philippians 4:8).

3. Guard your mouth. Say only what is uplifting, helpful, encouraging, true, and necessary.

4. Put on your Son-glasses and keep your eyes on Jesus, not the circumstances. Recognize that God has an eternal plan for your life and the lives of your friends.

As positive friends, let's take the precautions necessary to guard, protect, and nourish our most cherished relationships. For our friends' sakes as well as our own, let's choose to look at the circumstances of life from the perspective of God's faithfulness, power, and plan, rather than from our own limited viewpoint. Let's put on our Son-glasses and allow the beautiful light of God's love to warm our hearts and overflow into positive friendships with others.

POWER POINT

⚙ **Read:** Genesis 16:1–12; 21:1–20. Skim Luke 1:5–45 again. Four women, four babies—two different stories. What potential was there in these situations for the dark storm clouds of envy, bitterness, and gossip to build? How did each woman handle her situation? Which ladies wore their Son-glasses?

▽ **Pray:** Great and merciful Father, I rejoice in your unfailing love! It is filled with patience, kindness, goodness, and mercy. May these wonderful traits overflow in my words and actions toward others as I am refreshed by your love. Alert me to the seeds of envy, bitterness, or gossip that so easily crop up in my heart and mind. Keep me from destroying my friendships through my own anger or selfishness. Help me to always build up and never tear down those I love, as I depend on your Holy Spirit to work in and through me. In Jesus' name I pray, amen.

♀ **Remember:** "But now you must rid yourselves of all such things as these: anger, rage, malice, slander, and filthy language from your lips.... Therefore, as God's chosen people, holy and dearly loved, clothe yourselves with compassion, kindness, humility, gentleness and patience" (Colossians 3:8–12).

☺ **Do:** Stand up right now and walk to a mirror. Look boldly at your face in the glass, and then ask yourself if you have been guilty of gossip,

165

bitterness, or envy. Ask the Lord to help you see yourself clearly, then ask him to help you overcome whatever area of sin he reveals. Determine to seek forgiveness from others if necessary. Most importantly, repent. Turn from your destructive patterns, put on your Son-glasses, and choose to begin seeing things from an eternal perspective.

Cycles of Friendships
Tender Good-byes and Fresh Hellos

Be slow in choosing a friend, slower in changing.

—Benjamin Franklin

Do you remember the song that many of us sang as kids as we prepared to leave summer camp? We would gather with all the other campers and celebrate our newfound friendships with these lines: "Make new friends, but keep the old. One is silver and the other gold."

Comparing new friends to silver and old friends to gold sounds good. Silver and gold are precious metals, and our friendships are precious too. But the fact is, metals—even precious metals—can tarnish and rust. Silver, for example, turns dull and even black when not well maintained. A metal such as tin can rust to the point that the item fashioned out of it is no longer useful. Even gold can lose its luster as it gathers dust and grime over time. We know from experience that nearly two decades of hair spray can take a toll on a wedding ring.

Friendships are much like metal. They require maintenance if they are to retain their life-giving and soul-nurturing brilliance. We must take a long, hard look at our friendships to determine if they need to be polished up. It may be that a few of our relationships have begun to rust—some perhaps to the point that the friendship has been effectively rendered useless.

That old camp song brings up a question: Is it possible to maintain all of our old friendships while we build new ones? In the normal progression of life, we may be blessed with a few lifelong friends. But other friendships will come and go in the natural ebb and flow of living. Saying good-bye and releasing certain friendships is not necessarily a bad thing. Friendships have cycles. It's not that we hope for relationships to dissolve or weaken; but when they do naturally, we have more room in our lives for new friendships to blossom.

Proverbs 18:24 reminds us it is not necessarily a positive thing to have numerous friends: "A man of *too many* friends *comes* to ruin" (NASB). Why did Solomon write this? He was probably referring to the fact that the depth of a person's friendships is more important than the number of friends. As we mentioned in an earlier chapter, women with certain personalities are going to naturally tend to have many friends, simply because they never meet a stranger. But all of us can reach a point when we're juggling too many relationships. Attempting to maintain hundreds of good friends can be overwhelming. We end up running around trying in vain to please and serve everyone. We either become out-of-balance people and frazzled friends, or we relegate ourselves to carrying on surface friendships with no real quality or depth.

Sometimes women who have extremely large circles of acquaintances and friends are able to survive because they're like chameleons. As you know, a chameleon literally changes the color of its skin in order to blend in with different environments. Think back to your younger years. Like us, when you were between the ages of ten and seventeen, you probably knew certain girls who acted one way in front of one group of friends and another way in front of another group of friends.

They adjusted the way they walked and talked according to what they thought the group expected or demanded. In order to gain acceptance, they were not true to who they really were.

The sad thing is, some of these girls have grown up into insecure women who feel the need to garner a large number of friends, even at the expense of sacrificing their sense of self. In chapter 15 we will deal more with the concept of wearing "masks" in order to protect ourselves or hide our feelings. For now, suffice it to say that sacrificing who we are to acquire relationships comes with a high price tag. It can cause us to secure bonds of friendship that are unnecessary and perhaps even detrimental.

Our goal should be to develop deep, lasting, positive friendships—not simply gather a multitude of surface-level friends. As Ben Jonson, a contemporary of William Shakespeare, once said, "True happiness consists not in the multitude of friends, but in their worth and choice."[1] We need to find that delicate balance, that healthy flow, of the friendship cycle in our lives. We need to learn how and when to maintain certain friendships, release others, and develop new ones along life's journey.

That's what this chapter is about. We want to help you find the freedom to bring new friends into your life and, when necessary, release some old ones—even as you maintain a handful of those lifelong friendships that are so precious.

Circumstantial Cycles

Like it or not, circumstances do affect our friendships. Let's say you decide to work as a volunteer for a community service organization. On the first day you meet Anne, a woman who will be serving with you on a project. The two of you seem to "click" right off the bat, and for the next few weeks you talk on the phone every day about the tasks that must be accomplished. Over time you and Anne become friends, sharing more and more of the details of your lives. As you laugh together and work through challenges together, a bond is formed.

But then you finish the project, and your paths no longer cross on a regular basis. Will you remain good friends?

You may or you may not. It depends on the priority you (and Anne) have placed on the friendship. It would be very natural for the friendship to dissipate, and that wouldn't be a bad thing. You'd simply count Anne as a blessing for the time she was a part of your life. On the other hand, with a little effort, you could work to keep the relationship strong and vibrant. If you decide this is a friendship you want to maintain, then you need to set up a time—say, once a month—to get together or talk on the phone in order to "catch up."

Another circumstance that can change the dynamics of a friendship is a move. It's painful when a good friend or soul mate moves away.

❀

Karol reflects: I think about my friend Barbara. We shared a common desire to start a neighborhood Bible study. Barbara and I began praying, chatting, and planning how we might invite our neighbors to join the study. Before long we were meeting with a special group of ladies from the community, encouraging them and teaching them God's Word.

As you can imagine, Barbara and I became quite close as we worked, shared, and prayed together. Our friendship grew fast and deep. We were a team.

Then the inevitable happened.

Since Barbara's husband worked for a large corporation, the possi-

If a man does not make new acquaintances as he advances through life, he will soon find himself alone. A man, sir, should keep his friendships in constant repair. —Samuel Johnson

bility always existed that she would move away one day. And sure enough, the day came for her to move, and I knew our friendship would change. Barbara was a gift from God to me in many ways while she was here. She helped me through the birth of my daughters, Grace and Joy, and through the early years of parenting, since her kids were a little older and she had a nursing background. She inspired me and encouraged me as I taught the neighborhood Bible study and she handled the organizational details. She gave me courage and strength to reach out to my neighbors for Christ when I didn't have enough confidence to do it on my own.

At first Barb and I kept up through letters, occasional phone calls, and of course, Christmas cards. The years have brought many more moves for Barb, and we are "Christmas-card friends" at this point. She has a warm place in my heart, and I thank God for the blessing she has been in my life. There was a season for our close friendship. Yes, we probably could have worked harder at maintaining close contact, but the busyness of life pulled both of us in different directions. That happens. We need to be comfortable with the fact that all friendships are not meant to be lifelong. There's a natural cycle to friendships, and that's okay.

❁ ❁ ❁

Busyness itself can be an extenuating circumstance that causes some friendships to fade, become distant, or die. Perhaps you choose to take on additional responsibilities for a certain time period. A new child is born, or the pace of family life picks up. A new job requires you to travel. Sometimes busyness can't be helped, and friendships are naturally going to be affected. Other times, we fill our schedules with unnecessary time gobblers, crowding out meaningful time with those who are important to us. That kind of busyness *can* be helped. We need to make an ongoing self-assessment of our time management to be sure we're not pushing away friends unnecessarily.

Who am I pushing away?

Time to Say Good-bye

As much as we may not like the idea, however, there are times when deliberately ending a friendship is the right thing to do. Certain friends can be detrimental and even damaging to our lives. We must handle these cases with care; there's a thin line between sticking loyally with a person through thick and thin and cutting off an unhealthy relationship. So how do we know when it's the right time to say good-bye?

Before we answer that question, let's be clear: We are talking about friendships here—acquaintances, good friends, possibly even soul mates. We are *not* talking about marriages! Friendships can come and go, but a marriage is a covenant and a lifelong commitment between a husband and wife. Let's not confuse the two. Although certain situations may warrant a separation or divorce, we're not discussing those in this context. We're talking about our friendships with other women. And sometimes those friendships need to come to an end.

Friendship Thwarters

We can know that a friendship has become unhealthy and possibly detrimental when one of three "friendship thwarters" is present in the relationship:

1. An antiwisdom mind-set. Scripture and a realistic look at life point to the fact that there are two systems competing for our minds and hearts. The sinful system of this present world is diametrically opposed to the godly system for living spelled out in the Bible. In the words of Scripture we see the wisdom of God, which blesses and

172

fulfills our lives. But Scripture also makes clear that the ways of this world are unwise and foolish, ultimately bringing sorrow and destruction. They're the opposite of God's wisdom. We like to term this worldly mind-set "antiwisdom."

Unfortunately, antiwisdom can infect our friendships. Solomon gives us a hint about the damage a foolish, antiwisdom friend can inflict in Proverbs 13:20: "He who walks with the wise grows wise, but a companion of fools suffers harm." If we detect that a friend or companion is doing or saying foolish things that are opposed to the ways of God—if that friend appears to have no healthy fear of the Lord—we need to wise up! Foolish friends can lead us to do foolish things too.

Foolish friends give bad advice. They steer us the wrong way. They offer antiwisdom that works against God's moral principles and the wisdom from God's Word. Antiwisdom says, "Oh, don't worry about the consequences. You can do it just this once." Or, "You're too good for your husband. You deserve better. Have you considered a divorce?" If you have a foolish friend who constantly spouts this kind of antiwisdom, it's time to consider moving on.

2. A pattern of sin. Another friendship thwarter is an obvious pattern of sin in a friend's life. Such a friend has a history of making bad moral decisions and continues to choose a lifestyle of sin rather than righteousness. Of such friendships Paul said in 1 Corinthians 15:33, "Do not be misled: 'Bad company corrupts good character.'"

Typically, the bad corrupts the good. We wish it were the other way around! But more often than not, when we think, "I'll be a good influence on her," we're deceiving ourselves. Despite our best intentions, a bad companion can influence us to say and do things we may never have considered before.

Perhaps you're thinking, *But if I leave this friend, she'll have no good influences left in her life.* If you sense that the person needs your help

A man of many companions may come to ruin, but there is a friend who sticks closer than a brother.
—Proverbs 18:24

but may not be open to encouragement in the right direction, by all means, have a relationship; just keep it at arm's length. Stay in touch but don't run around together like best buddies.

3. *A tendency to enable. Enable* is a popular word right now. It means to play a part or even encourage another person to continue in a destructive addiction or lifestyle. If you detect that a friend is using you to reinforce a wrong behavior, you need to put a halt to the situation. Tough love is in order. You may need to separate yourself from this friend and then provide godly counsel or wisdom only from a distance. In other words, you may need to stop socializing with this person and only contact her with one purpose in mind: to encourage her to make wise choices.

In some situations, a friendship must be severed for a time—with that severing coming in the form of a necessary intervention. Consider the following true story:

Cathy, Melanie, and Chris were friends. Since their children went to the same school, they shared carpooling duties in the mornings and afternoons. For years the carpool worked without a hitch. Then Chris began making excuses about why she was going to be late to pick up the kids on a particular day. Sometimes she wouldn't show up at all, leaving the children to wait until the school secretary called one of the other moms to come and get them.

The truth finally came out when her friends' patience had been worn thin: Chris, an alcoholic who had been sober for over seventeen years, had started to drink again. Her addiction had gotten to the point that she was beginning to pass out in the afternoons. Sometimes she didn't even realize it was time for the children to get out of school. On one particular day she showed up at school intoxicated and insisted that the children get in the car. Thankfully the teachers in charge of school pickup wouldn't allow the children to ride with her.

As soon as Cathy and Melanie realized what was going on, they quit carpooling with Chris. But day after day, week after week, Chris would leave her eleven-year-old, Dustin, at school without a ride home. At the last minute she would call Cathy or Melanie; and day after day, week after week, one of the two friends would come to the rescue. After all, they figured, it wasn't Dustin's fault. On certain rare days, Chris would show up to pick up her little guy, and she would appear to be perfectly fine. But most days she would depend on Cathy and Melanie to get Dustin.

For the longest time, the two friends were compliant, concerned about Chris but happy to help. Finally, enough was enough. They told Chris they would no longer bring Dustin home. They also called Chris's husband, Eric, at his office and filled him in on what had been going on for over two months. Chris was furious. Amazingly, she had kept her little secret from her husband up to that point. His job required him to travel a great deal, so he hadn't been around enough to notice what was wrong.

"How could you betray my confidence like that?" she cried.

But Cathy and Melanie were not apologetic. They realized they had been enabling Chris's irresponsible and dangerous behavior for weeks. Thankfully, they put an end to the enablement and forced Chris to get the help she needed, even though it cost them a severed relationship.

We never want to use the fear of enabling as an excuse to not help someone in need. On the other hand, we need to be sure we're helping in a wise and prudent way. We may need to force a break in the relationship if we detect that a friend is dependent on us in ways that are unhealthy.

How to Say Good-bye

Let's say you recognize that a particular friend is a negative and destructive influence in your life. How are you going to tell her in love that it's time to say good-bye? Here are four steps to help you close out an unhealthy friendship:

1. *Begin distancing yourself.* Don't call to chat; don't invite her to lunch; don't plan to get together. This will begin to provide a natural break for releasing the relationship.

2. *Plan a brief statement explaining why you feel it's best that you not hang out together.* Don't attempt this without seeking the Lord in prayer. Ask him to give you the words to say. Ask him to help you be humble, loving, truthful, and firm. You might say something like this: "Jenny, I appreciate many things about our friendship, but lately I've become increasingly uncomfortable with the negative comments you continue to make about my marriage. Marriage is hard at times; but I am committed to working things out with Jim, and you don't seem to support me in this. Although I like you, I just can't spend time with you right now. I think it's best that we don't get together as often."

3. *Decide if this message needs to be delivered directly or simply kept on hand, ready to use.* Different relationships call for different methods. You need to discern if the situation calls for a direct encounter and an explicit good-bye, or if the relationship can be allowed to simply die a slow, silent death. In some cases, it's hard to know which way to go. Always be ready with the message you formed in step 2.

4. *Keep it short and simple.* The more words you use, the more likely you are to get yourself into trouble, dig yourself into a hole, or find yourself in an argument. Don't add a bunch of "I'm sorrys" or go on

and on trying to explain your explanations. Stay concise and to the point, keeping a loving but firm tone.

The Goal

As we bring this chapter to a close, we want to remind you that our goal has not been to encourage you to say good-bye to relationships; rather, it's been to help you recognize the beautiful cycles of friendship we all have in our lives. In a garden you find a variety of flowers. Some are annuals. They are there for a time and a season. They have a purpose and a place. They add beauty and color to our lives for a brief period, just as some friends add joy to our lives for a season. Other flowers are perennials. They bloom year after year. They may lay dormant for a while, but then they return to life and blossom all over again. Like certain friends, they are faithful and true.

Weeds also crop up in a garden, often appearing at first as beautiful, blossoming flowers. Before long, however, they lose their eye appeal and begin to encroach upon the rest of the vegetation, choking the very life out of other healthy, growing things. Such is the way with a friendship gone bad. We need to take time to weed our friendship gardens by assessing our relationships often. Taking time to "weed and feed" is what makes a garden a wonderful sight to behold!

Sometimes flowers emerge through the planting of seeds that we nurture to full growth over time. Other times flowers are planted in full blossom. Either way, the result is beautiful. Friendships can be like that. In some of our most meaningful friendships, an acquaintance blossoms into a vibrant, heart-to-heart soul mate over many years of steady nurture. In other close relationships, we're instantly drawn together because a common interest or incident has caused our hearts to be entwined.

By nature a garden is in constant flux. The new comes in and the old fades out, hopefully as a sweet memory. Friendships have a similar harmonious cycle. Let's be comfortable with the changes, always cultivating the growth of new, positive friendships while maintaining the beauty and vitality of the older, lifelong ones.

And while we're at it, let's remember to pick the weeds in order for our friendship garden to be vibrantly healthy and fragrant.

POWER POINT

Read: Acts 15:36–39. What do you discover about Paul and Barnabas? Was God's work thwarted? Have you ever personally encountered a Paul-and-Barnabas-type situation where you agreed to disagree? Read Colossians 4:10 and Philemon 1:24 to see how it worked out.

Pray: Oh, wonderful Lord, thank you for the seasons of life. Thank you for the fresh springtime of new growth. Thank you for the harvest. You are a renewing and redeeming God, and I praise you for the beauty of your work! Thank you also for the seasons of friendship and for the beautiful garden of friends you have planted in my life. Help me to graciously work through the natural changes that take place in this garden. Give me the discernment to know when a friend is causing me harm and the courage and wisdom to say good-bye if necessary. Most importantly, help me to enjoy the positive friends you place in my life, whether our time together is long or short. In Jesus' name, amen.

Remember: "A man of many companions may come to ruin, but there is a friend who sticks closer than a brother" (Proverbs 18:24).

Do: Reflect on some of the relationships that have come in and out of your life over the years, and take a moment to pray for those special friends who were with you for a season. Now reflect on your current friendships. Are there some that need to fade away because they are negative or unhealthy? Are there some budding relationships that need to be nurtured? Have you been fretting because you are not as close to a particular friend as you once were? Release that relationship to God and ask the Lord for direction in that friendship as well as in others.

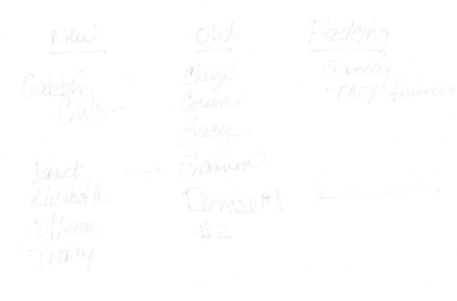

Power Principle #5

THe P●wer OF Spiritual b●nds

*We have heard of your faith in Christ Jesus
and of the love you have for all the saints.*

—Colossians 1:4

May the Lord make your love increase and overflow for each other and for everyone else, just as ours does for you. May he strengthen your hearts so that you will be blameless and holy in the presence of our God and Father when our Lord Jesus comes with all his holy ones.

—1 Thessalonians 3:12–13

Faith-Filled Friends
The Sweet Fellowship of Believers

Dear Lord, my friends have been to me
Interpreters of love divine,
And in their kindness I have seen
Thine everlasting mercy shine!

—Martha Shell Nicholson

Bible study and prayer were the marks of Barbara Kinder's life. She was a loving wife, devoted mother, and very proud grandmother. Her friends knew her as a prayer warrior. Although she did not enjoy speaking in front of people, when she was asked to be an assistant teaching leader for a local Bible Study Fellowship group, she prayerfully accepted. It was a faith step for Barbara, but she loved God's Word and trusted him for the ability to share it. Most of Barbara's dearest friendships were born from her involvement in BSF.

One friend from Bible study (also named Barbara) became her prayer partner. The two Barbaras met faithfully every single week and prayed about every—and we mean *every*—aspect of their lives. The husbands and children of these two women knew they were being faithfully prayed for through every event of their lives, from making speeches to taking tests.

A vigorous morning walk was a part of Barbara Kinder's everyday routine. She went for several miles early in the morning, and she loved to use this time to pray. Typically she would see several ladies along the walking path who seemed to walk every day at the same time.

Eventually they asked Barbara to join them. For many of us, that would be an easy yes, because we would enjoy the company. But for Barbara the invitation was a bit of a dilemma, because she loved to walk and talk to the Lord.

As she took the matter to prayer, she felt that the Lord was urging her to walk with the other ladies and share God's love with them. She didn't know exactly where they stood spiritually, but she realized she was being offered a great opportunity to communicate God's love and truth. So she told the women yes. And thus began a wonderful journey of sharing about family, friends, and faith with the morning walkers for the next several years.

There were certain mornings when Barbara needed to take her walk a little earlier than the rest of the ladies. These were the days she attended Bible study and needed to prepare for class. The morning of October 31, 1990, was one of those mornings. Barbara got up early, read from her favorite devotional, *My Utmost for His Highest* by Oswald Chambers, then headed out the door while it was still dark and began walking. She was on the last stretch of her walk and heading for home as the early morning light dawned. Barbara knew she needed to put the final touches on her Bible lesson; it was her turn to teach the group of over one hundred ladies at BSF.

As Barbara reached La Manga Street (just a small, two-lane road) she saw an SUV at the stop sign. She assumed the driver also saw her. He did not. For whatever reason, as she began to cross the street, he moved forward. He didn't even realize he had hit someone until he heard a scream.

A typically gentle and careful driver had made an unusual error, and Barbara Kinder lay on the street, her body hurt and bleeding. The driver stopped, and people—mostly other joggers and walkers—began gathering. Barbara was dying.

Interestingly, everyone at the scene distinctly remembers seeing a silver-haired man (not the driver of the SUV) holding Barbara and stroking her bleeding head as she took her final breaths. Bystanders said they had never seen a person demonstrate so much compassion and mercy. But the silver-haired man was never seen or heard from after the accident. Some say he was an angel. Others, a doctor. Whoever he was, he was most certainly God's loving and tender provision for Barbara during her last moments.

Barbara had often told her family, "I hope that when the Lord is ready to take me home, he does it quickly. I don't want to linger and be a burden to anyone." God allowed this saintly woman to die in the manner she desired. Those of us left behind on earth felt it was too early for her to leave us. But for Barbara, her death was simply an early home-going and reward.

The announcement was made at BSF that Barbara Kinder had gone home to be with the Lord that morning. The speaker read a quote from Barbara's daughter that said, "Mother loved to pray and walk. I suppose she was having a great conversation with God then had a little interruption and finished her conversation face to face." The women at the Bible study were comforted by the knowledge that Barbara was, without a doubt, in the presence of the Lord.

Barbara's husband, Garry, was out of town when the accident occurred. As soon as he heard the news, he began working feverishly to find a return flight home. Meanwhile Barbara's daughters manned the home front as friends began streaming to the Kinders' house to offer their love and support.

Although Barbara was a humble, behind-the-scenes type of person, she was rich with friends. The funeral a few days later was a testimony to a godly woman and a blessing to all who attended. The large auditorium filled up as people from church, BSF, and the community came to pay tribute. And over the days and weeks that followed, Garry received hundreds upon hundreds of cards and letters from people telling how Barbara had blessed them with the love and kindness of God.

By his wife's bedside, Garry found the devotional book that Barbara had been reading the very morning she died. The devotion for that day was based on a scripture found in Job 13:15: "Though he slay me, yet will I hope in him." Certainly Barbara's hope was in her everlasting Lord. Her life was built on her faith in him. Her closest friendships were based on a common love for him. God was her all in all.

❀

Karol reflects: I can tell you this story about Barbara Kinder with a depth of love, respect, and emotion, because Barbara Kinder was my mother. I am continually blessed by the spiritual foundation she laid in my life, and I am equally as blessed to see how her faith influenced other people. To this day, more than a decade later, people still mention to me how much they loved and appreciated my mother. She was a faith-filled friend.

❀ ❀ ❀

A Life of Faith

Oh, the power of faith! It colors how we look at our world and gives us purpose beyond measure. It draws us together with others in sweet and precious fellowship as friends. There is no deeper bond we can share with another person than the bond of faith in Christ.

What about you? Where are you in your journey of faith? We can relate the levels of friendship that we learned about in chapter 3 to the levels of our relationship with God. Consider where you fit in the following three categories.

God's Acquaintances

Many people have heard about Jesus. They celebrate his birthday at Christmas and his resurrection at Easter, but they only know *about* him; they don't really know him. They may even go to church on Sundays, but they have never drawn close to God in a meaningful relationship. To them, God is an acquaintance. They acknowledge that he exists, but they don't go much further.

Jesus speaks about this kind of acquaintance-level relationship in Matthew 7:21–23, which is part of the Sermon on the Mount. He exposes those people who appear religious but who don't really have a relationship with him. Here is the passage in the New Living Translation:

> Not all people who sound religious are really godly. They may refer to me as "Lord," but they still won't enter the Kingdom of Heaven. The decisive issue is whether they obey my Father in heaven. On judgment day many will tell me, "Lord, Lord, we prophesied in your name and cast out demons in your name and performed many miracles in your name." But I will reply, "I never knew you. Go away; the things you did were unauthorized (unlawful)."

Wow! Get the picture? God wants us to know him, not just play the games that make us look like we know him. To know God is to have a relationship with him beyond the acquaintance level.

God's Good Friends

At some point we may have an aha moment with an acquaintance that moves this person into the precious fold of good friendship. A relationship is born. In a similar way, we may start out knowing about Jesus; but at some aha moment, we realize that he is

We ought always to thank God for you, brothers, and rightly so, because your faith is growing more and more, and the love every one of you has for each other is increasing. —2 Thessalonians 1:3

☺

more than a distant God. He is the lover of our souls. He took the form of human flesh to offer his life for us on the cross and to rise again, giving us hope for eternal life. We enter into a relationship with this loving God when we take a step of faith and trust our hearts and lives to him.

Jesus calls us to be more than Sunday acquaintances. He calls us to be his friends, to walk with him day by day. Let's sit in on a session Jesus had with his disciples on the night of the Last Supper and hear what he had to say about friendship with him:

> If you obey my commands, you will remain in my love, just as I have obeyed my Father's commands and remain in his love. I have told you this so that my joy may be in you and that your joy may be complete. My command is this: Love each other as I have loved you. Greater love has no one than this, that he lay down his life for his friends. You are my friends if you do what I command. I no longer call you servants, because a servant does not know his master's business. Instead, I have called you friends, for everything that I learned from my Father I have made known to you. (John 15:10–15)

Clearly, Jesus wants to have more than a casual relationship with us. His intention is that we enter into a relationship of close fellowship with him through faith, by abiding in him through obedience.

Have you come to that aha moment in your life with Christ? Have you placed your faith and trust in Jesus and moved into a relationship with him that goes deeper than the acquaintance level? If not, why not take this moment to begin that deeper relationship? Thank him for coming to earth to die for your sins and ask him to forgive you and help you to walk in obedience to him. Tell him you believe he died and rose again, giving you the promise of eternal life.

Consider what James had to say about the Old Testament patriarch, Abraham: "The scripture was fulfilled that says, 'Abraham believed God, and it was credited to him as righteousness,' and he was called God's friend" (James 2:23). As we believe God, take a step of faith into a deeper relationship, and walk in obedience to him day by day, we are his friends too.

God's Soul Mates

The most fulfilling friendships are found at the level of intimacy attained between true soul mates. In John 15:5–9, Jesus encourages this deeper level of friendship between him and his followers:

> I am the vine; you are the branches. If a man remains in me and I in him, he will bear much fruit; apart from me you can do nothing. If anyone does not remain in me, he is like a branch that is thrown away and withers; such branches are picked up, thrown into the fire and burned. If you remain in me and my words remain in you, ask whatever you wish, and it will be given you. This is to my Father's glory, that you bear much fruit, showing yourselves to be my disciples.
>
> As the Father has loved me, so have I loved you. Now remain in my love.

How do we remain in Jesus' love? The word *remain* can also be translated, "abide, dwell, live in." Each day, moment by moment, we can abide, dwell, and live in Christ by praying and dwelling on his Word, the Bible. Brother Lawrence, the seventeenth-century monk, called this "practicing His presence." Personally we've found it helpful to memorize Bible verses so we can literally carry his Word with us wherever we go. That's why we suggest a verse to remember in the Power Point at the end of each chapter. As we walk in obedience to

God, spend time with him in prayer, and listen to him as he speaks to us through his Word, our relationship with him grows more and more intimate and deep. We actually become soul mates with the almighty God of the universe!

True Fellowship

Fellowship is what friends experience together when their faith connects them. True fellowship with other believers draws us into deep and lasting relationships, because we share a common eternal bond. Not only do our minds connect with other Christians, but our hearts and souls do too. Our interest in one another goes beyond the surface level to eternal issues that really matter.

❧

Karol reflects: Terry Ann and I experienced this kind of fellowship in our own friendship, starting in our college days. We are truly spiritual sisters. Throughout our lives, God has brought us other spiritual friends, too, who have helped and encouraged us on the journey of faith.

❧ ❧ ❧

The Bible Connection

How does a relationship of this nature get started? In Barbara Kinder's case, her closest friends developed through her involvement in Bible studies. As Christians we can't help but connect with other women when we study the Bible together and apply the rich treasure of God's Word to our lives on a regular basis.

How do you find a Bible study that is right for you? You may want to begin by looking in your own church first. Does it support one or more women's Bible study groups? If so, joining a group may

Chapter 12: Faith-Filled Friends

be a great way to interact with new friends beyond brief Sunday hellos and good-byes.

Next, consider checking out a national Bible study organization that may have group studies in your community. We mentioned Bible Study Fellowship earlier when we talked about Barbara. Community Bible Study and Kay Arthur's *Precept upon Precept* also offer excellent opportunities to grow in God's Word with friends. Most of these studies offer night groups for working men and women as well as the typical day groups. Many, many lasting friendships have been birthed in groups such as these. They require faithful attendance and homework during the week, but the effort is well worth it, and hearts are easily drawn together.

Another organization that brings women together in the fellowship of Christ is Christian Women's Clubs, organized by Stonecroft Ministries. This outstanding organization offers once-a-month luncheons with interesting speakers as well as small-group Bible studies and prayer circles. You can find a Christian Women's Club in most communities. Go to stonecroft.org to find one near you.

We also recommend Moms in Touch, a wonderful organization that draws together women whose children attend the same school. The moms meet together weekly at an off-campus location in order to pray for the needs of the children, the school faculty, and the administration. Check the Moms in Touch Web site (www.momsintouch.org) to see if a group has already been formed for your child's school. If not, consider starting one.

Many deep friendships can grow in an environment of common prayer. Both of us have several friends with whom we get together one-on-one on a semiregular basis to pray about our activities and the needs of our families. We've also had seasons when a circle of friends has joined together to meet on a regular basis to pray.

Karol reflects: When my friend Pam needed prayer for her daughter with Crohn's disease, Dana, Susan, Carol, and I began meeting with her on a weekly basis to pray. As time went on, new issues arose, and the group continued to pray together for a multitude of needs, hurts, and concerns. Not only did we have the joy of seeing answered prayer together, but we also grew to have a deep and abiding love for one another. We trusted each other with some of the most intimate details of our lives because we were going to the heavenly Father together.

The Encouragement Connection

Friends in the faith are the greatest source of encouragement this world has to offer. The apostle Paul was an encourager, and he implored the early Christians to be encouragers too. Notice his words in 1 Thessalonians 5:9–11: "For God did not appoint us to suffer wrath but to receive salvation through our Lord Jesus Christ. He died for us so that, whether we are awake or asleep, we may live together with him. Therefore encourage one another and build each other up, just as in fact you are doing."

Because our hope is in the Lord Jesus Christ and the salvation he provides, we are a people of hope who can encourage one another with God's Word, God's comfort, and God's strength. We have a connection with other believers that goes beyond any normal worldly connection. It's a heart connection, because our hearts are bent together toward the Lord and his work.

The story is told of an American doctor who was traveling in Korea and knew barely enough of the language to get by. On one particular day, when he was riding on a train, an old Korean man boarded and sat down across from him. The old man carried a bundle of white cloth. Soon the old man began talking to the doctor, pouring out an abundance of words that the doctor could not understand.

Finally the doctor spoke up with one of the few Korean sentences he had memorized. Translated it meant, "I do not understand Korean." But the old man persisted in conversation, and the doctor persisted equally in repeating his sentence.

In the Korean man's river of words, the doctor noticed one word that seemed familiar. Was the old man saying something about Jesus? All doubt vanished when the man pointed to the doctor and asked, "Yesu? Yesu?" The doctor nodded and smiled in agreement, saying, "Yesu, Yesu."

The old man beamed from ear to ear as he opened his bundle of cloth and proudly displayed a Korean Bible. Then he lovingly opened his treasured Bible and put his finger on a verse. Of course the doctor couldn't read it, but he turned in his own Bible to the same place and read 1 John 3:14: "We know that we have passed from death unto life, because we love the brethren" (KJV).[1]

Clearly there is no greater bond than the one believers have in Christ. It transcends all natural and human barriers—language included!

The Faith Connection

Friends in the Lord are true gifts. They offer more than friendship; they offer eternal hope and an eternal perspective. We need to ask ourselves, *Are we being this kind of friend to others? Are we encouraging our friends in their faith on a regular basis? Do we talk about our delight in the Lord all week long, or do we reserve such conversations for Sunday mornings only? When our friends are struggling, do we remind them of God's unfailing love and care? Do we know how to offer comfort through a Bible verse or prayer?*

The key to being a positive spiritual friend is making sure our own faith is vibrant and ever deepening. When our faith is living and active, we naturally connect with others in the faith. And as we continue to build our relationship with Christ, we are able to build deep and lasting bonds with other sisters in Christ as he works in our lives.

We close with a poem by Anne Peters that reflects the depth of the spiritual bond we share with other believers in Christ.

Sisters in Christ

You are my sister, this I know, for the Father tells me so.

Your loving kindness in my life has been to me a sacrifice.

You took the time to help me through the terrible pain that I once knew.

This sisterhood that we do share shows how much our God does care.

You are my sister, this I know, for the Father tells me so.

He sent to us His perfect plan so we could stand here hand in hand.

But more amazing is His love that changed our hearts to be as one.

He sent you to me in His name and never will I be the same.

You are my sister, this I know, for the Father tells me so.

Thank you for the love you have shown so the Father can be known.

It's in all the little things that we do glimpse what heaven brings—

A crown of glory from above to reward a sister's love.

You are my sister, this I know, for the Father tells me so.

His precious Son did pay the price, so we could be sisters in Christ![2]

POWER POINT

⚙ **Read:** Colossians 3:12–17; 4:2–18. What traits do you see in these verses that describe true Christian love and fellowship? What do you notice about the greetings Paul expresses at the end of chapter 4? What characteristics of Christian fellowship do you see in your own life?

♡ **Pray:** Glorious Lord, you are my strength and salvation. My hope is in you! Thank you for allowing mankind to have a relationship with you through Jesus. Thank you that because of Jesus I can draw close to you. Help me to abide in you through your Word and prayer each day. Thank you also for my faith-filled friends. May our friendships continue to deepen over time as we encourage one another and build each other up in the journey of faith. Use me to inspire my friends spiritually and comfort them emotionally. Thank you for the deep bond we have based on our mutual faith in you. In Jesus' name I pray, amen.

💡 **Remember:** "Let the word of Christ dwell in you richly as you teach and admonish one another with all wisdom" (Colossians 3:16).

☺ **Do:** Take a step of faith to draw closer to God. Determine to abide in him by setting aside a regular time for personal prayer and reading the Bible. If you're not a part of a Bible study or fellowship group, begin looking for one that you can join, or start a prayer group that fits your schedule. Look for other believers with whom you can connect through your mutual love for the Lord.

Paul offers a strategy to live day by day
(1) compassion, forgiveness (2) love guides your life
(3) peace of Christ Rule in your heart, (4) always thankful
(5) God's word in you C all times, (6) live as a JC Representative

13

Living It Out
Creative Ways to Express the Love of Christ

I would not give much for your religion unless it can be seen.
Lamps do not talk, but they do shine.

—Charles H. Spurgeon

In 1984, Home Sweet Home Records released *Vital Signs,* an album by the Christian band WhiteHeart. Tucked away on side two of the album is a song titled "We Are His Hands." It poetically describes the truth that we are to reflect the Spirit of Christ in a tangible and physical way to those individuals who pass in and out of our lives. The oft-quoted expression "Our lives may be the only Bible some people ever read" is so very true. People all around us are hurting, and they desperately need a touch from the Master's hand. They don't want to be lectured about the sin in their lives that caused their hurt and pain unless the person doing the lecturing has first loved them in their neediness. Authentic love cares more about the person than the lifestyle the person leads.

So often we underestimate the power of a smile, a hug, a genuine compliment, undivided attention, or the smallest act of kindness. All of these acts of love have the potential to turn a life around. Consider this story, which we recently received in an e-mail.

A little boy wanted to meet God. He knew it was a long trip to where God lived, so he packed his suitcase with Twinkies and a six-pack of root beer and started his journey. When he had gone about three blocks, he saw an old man sitting alone in the park, staring at some pigeons. The boy sat down next to the man and opened his suitcase. He was about to take a drink of root beer when he noticed that the old man looked hungry, so he handed him a Twinkie.

The old man gratefully accepted the treat and smiled at the boy. His smile was so pleasant that the boy wanted to see it again, so he handed him a root beer. Again the old man smiled at him. The boy was delighted! The two ended up sitting on the bench all afternoon, eating and smiling but never saying a word.

As it grew dark, the boy realized that he was tired. He got up to leave, but before he had gone more than a few steps, he turned around, ran back to the old man, and hugged him. The old man gave him his biggest smile ever.

When the boy opened the door to his own house a short time later, his mother was surprised by the look of joy on his face.

"What did you do today that made you so happy?" she asked.

"I had lunch with God," the boy said. And before his mother could respond, he added, "You know what? He's got the most beautiful smile I've ever seen!"

Meanwhile, the old man, also radiant with joy, returned to his home. His son was stunned by the look of peace on his father's face.

"Dad, what did you do today that made you so happy?" the son asked.

"I ate Twinkies in the park with God," the old man said. And before his son could respond, he added, "You know, he's much younger than I expected."[1]

What does God look like? We're not exactly sure, but we do know this: We should look like him! The old expression "Like father, like son" described Jesus perfectly. Of course, he literally was God in the flesh, so looking like God came naturally to him. We, on the other hand, are not God; and on our own, in our own strength, we don't even closely resemble our heavenly Father. We must allow God, by his Holy Spirit, to live through us. Then, just like Jesus, we can have the heart of God—and the smile of God that brightens the world for everyone around us.

God's Power Working through Us

An incident recorded in Mark 9:14–29 gives us insight into our responsibility as Christ-followers to touch lives for God. Jesus, Peter, James, and John had just returned from a "mountaintop experience" (the Transfiguration!) to find the other disciples arguing with teachers of the Jewish law. When Jesus asked his disciples, "What are you arguing about?" a man in the crowd responded, "Teacher, I brought you my son, who is possessed by a spirit.…I asked your disciples to drive out the spirit, but they could not" (vv. 17–18).

Jesus immediately drove the spirit out of the boy. Later his disciples asked him privately why they hadn't been able to do it. Jesus replied, "This kind can come out only by prayer" (v. 29).

Apparently the disciples had failed to recognize that the power to touch lives was not inherent in them. It was a power that was granted to them by God and given to them through prayer. Like the disciples, without prayer we are rendered powerless to impact others. But when we start our days by spending time with God, life is rarely mundane. Our ears, eyes, and hearts become more in tune with the needs of the people around us. We're better able to discern when our husbands and children and friends are troubled. We're more open to acquaintances and even strangers we meet and therefore more willing to say a kind word or lend a listening ear.

Have you ever been in prayer and had a friend's name come to

199

mind for no apparent reason—and when you call her you discover that she really needed an encouraging word from a caring friend at that moment? That is so like God! He always meets us at our point of need, and many times he uses one of his children to extend his loving embrace.

Enjoying the company of God through prayer and the study of his Word will start us on a journey that can be positively life altering—for us and for the people whose lives we touch. But if we're going to have the impact that God intends, we must quit being people-pleasers and start being God-pleasers. We must be willing to step out of our comfort zones when God tells us to. We must be willing to listen to God's quiet nudging, look beyond our own self-interests, and reach out to others.

Terry Ann reflects: Recently I went with my sister Julie to a boutique to see a dress that she was thinking about purchasing. While she was in the fitting room, the sales clerk approached me, and I told her I was Julie's sister.

"I have to tell you how your sister greatly impacted someone's life," the woman said.

Of course I was all ears. The clerk proceeded to tell me that when Julie was browsing in the store several days earlier, another customer was shopping there too. The customer was frail and had lost most of her hair. Julie struck up a conversation, and the woman explained that she was battling cancer.

In the course of their conversation, the woman said that she admired the bracelet that Julie was wearing—a beautiful piece of jewelry adorned with brilliant crystals. Julie thanked her for the compliment and continued to visit with her a little more.

Later, as the woman prepared to leave the store, Julie took off her bracelet and discreetly placed it in her new friend's hand. "I'll be praying for you," Julie said.

The sales clerk smiled as she told me the story. Then she added, "That woman came back in the store just yesterday in hopes that I would know your sister's name. She wanted to be able to thank her. She said that for the first time in a long time, she had hope."

Julie was Jesus for that woman that day.

❧ ❧ ❧

Not for Our Glory

The Bible says that the Lord rewards the good things that we do in secret. In Matthew 6:1–4 we read,

> Be careful not to do your "acts of righteousness" before men, to be seen by them. If you do, you will have no reward from your Father in heaven. So when you give to the needy, do not announce it with trumpets, as the hypocrites do in the synagogues and on the streets, to be honored by men. I tell you the truth, they have received their reward in full. But when you give to the needy, do not let your left hand know what your right hand is doing, so that your giving may be in secret. Then your Father, who sees what is done in secret, will reward you.

How easy is it for us to help someone when we know we're going to receive credit or glory for our stupendous acts of service! It's much harder to bless someone in secret, knowing that God is the only one who will see what we do.

Recently, an interesting episode of *Spy TV* aired in our area. In one particular segment, actors dressed as limousine drivers pulled up in a black stretch limousine to a randomly chosen house in a typical suburban neighborhood. They walked up to the door and knocked. When the homeowner came to the door, the drivers said they had a very famous movie star in the car who really needed to use the bathroom. He couldn't wait any longer, they said. Of course the homeowner was not only obliging but in awe of the fact that this famous person wanted to enter his home and use the facilities!

In a roundabout way, the show pointed out that we all tend to be "respecters of persons." If an unknown, ordinary "Joe" had just popped in to use the facilities, the homeowner might not have been so hospitable. In other words, we feel that certain people really are more valuable, more important, or more significant than others.

This concept is diametrically opposed to the teachings of Christ. One time when Jesus was traveling with his disciples, he heard them arguing among themselves. When he asked what they were arguing about, the Scripture says that "they kept quiet because on the way they had argued about who was the greatest" (Mark 9:34). Doesn't that sound a lot like the bickering that goes on in our homes and churches? Jesus responded by saying, "If anyone wants to be first, he must be the very last, and the servant of all" (v. 35). Then he called a little child to come over to him. Holding the child in his arms, he continued, "Whoever welcomes one of these little children in my name welcomes me; and whoever welcomes me does not welcome me but the one who sent me" (v. 37).

Jesus couldn't have been any clearer. Don't you know his disciples hung their heads in shame? Shouldn't we all? How often do we seek to please only the "right" kind of people? How often do we try to make a good impression on those we view as having a high social standing?

Recently we heard a wonderful story about one of our nation's top-ranking government officials. He was attending a fundraiser when

All right believing in God is visibly reflected in right behavior towards men. —Geoffrey B. Wilson

he was approached by a woman and her teenage son. The woman told the official that she was a Christian and that she was praying for him as he worked on behalf of the citizens.

The official looked at the woman's son and asked, "Are you a believer too?" When the teenager answered that he wasn't sure, the official asked if he could talk with him for a few minutes about the Lord. He then proceeded to lead the young man to Christ. Amazing, isn't it? This national leader put his "important" event and "important" people aside in order to do what Jesus commanded: to "welcome one of these little children in my name." He showed himself to be a true leader because he looked to serve, not to be served. He didn't look to receive glory; he looked to serve the God of glory.

Leaving a Legacy

Writing this book has brought back memory after memory of our parents teaching us the importance of living out our faith in such a way that people would be drawn to the love of Christ they see demonstrated in us. We want to be sure to pass this legacy on to our own children. We both feel strongly that we must leave more to our children than simply a financial statement! Above all else we want to leave them an example of a faith lived out in service to others, just as our parents did for us.

❀

Terry Ann reflects: When I was in college my father experienced a huge setback in his career. Of course it couldn't have come at a better time. *Not!* Mom and Dad were attempting to put my two sisters and me through college, and Dad's work situation was now forcing him to live and work in another city. This meant he had to spend a great deal of time away from my mother during this difficult period of financial struggle. Daddy was literally living in his out-of-town office, because he couldn't afford to pay for two residences.

Periodically Dad would visit a local Christian bookstore to browse. One day he noticed a beautifully framed picture that captured his mind and heart. It was a large print of a grief-stricken businessman sitting at his desk with his face in his hands. The newspaper was lying open on his desk. Perhaps he had lost everything in a stock market crash. Perhaps he had lost his family. Whatever his grief, it was great. But there kneeling at his feet was Jesus. Jesus, our Lord and Comforter, was washing the feet of this businessman whose life was in shambles.

Daddy wanted the picture, but given the financial pressure he was under, he knew he couldn't spend the two-hundred-plus dollars to purchase it. So from time to time he would go to the store just to reflect on it. It brought him peace in the midst of his own personal trial.

On one particular visit to the store, a young sales clerk came up to Dad and asked, "Can I help you?"

"No," he answered, "I'm simply here to admire this picture."

She nodded and stood beside him. "I like to stare at the picture every day. It gives me strength," she said.

"Why?" asked my father, who never meets a stranger.

She began to share her story. She and her husband had two young children, and she had always stayed home to care for them. But a year ago her husband had lost his job. Now she was working at the Christian bookstore, trying to make enough money to keep them from losing their home.

Meanwhile, her husband had lost hope. Nearly every time he'd gone for a job interview, he'd been told that his only drawback was that he was overqualified. Month after month of rejection had left him in despair. He no longer even desired to try to find work. Their marriage and family were falling apart.

When the clerk finished telling her tearful story, she thanked Dad for letting her cry on the shoulder of a stranger. Then she turned to busy herself with another customer. That's when Dad heard the voice of the Lord deep in his heart. Obediently he slipped over to the checkout counter and, in a hushed voice, asked another sales associate to ring up the picture for him. Then, with tears in his eyes, he presented the picture as a gift to the young woman, asking her to give it to her husband.

"He needs to know that the Lord not only cares about him; he has a plan for his life," Dad explained.

The woman couldn't believe it. A complete stranger—someone who also was in need—was blessing her at just the time she needed it most! Dad didn't want any credit or praise, because he knew he'd only done what God instructed him to do. By sacrificially purchasing the anointed piece of art, he'd been obedient to the voice of God.

My father was so quiet about the incident that I didn't find out about it until several years later, when my mom shared the story with me. But what a deep impact his compassion and obedience made on my life! I want to touch lives like that, don't you?

❀

Karol reflects: My mother was a gifted seamstress (a lost art in today's society). She made many of our clothes when my sisters and I were young. I still remember all the trying moments—punctuated with cries of "Stand still!"—that took place as she pinned up hems or fitted seams for new dresses she was making for us.

I remember one summer in particular when Mother used her sewing talent to express God's love and compassion. I was in my early teens, and I noticed that my mother was sewing a new dress. I didn't recognize it as one she was making for our family, so I questioned her about it.

"Some of the young people at the orphanage need new dresses," she told me, "and I'm sewing several to give to them."

I'll never forget the joy I felt one Sunday when one of the girls from the orphanage bounced into my Sunday school class wearing a dress my mother had made! She looked beautiful and appeared more confident than I'd ever seen her. A warm and wonderful feeling came over me as I realized my mother had played a part in making this girl feel honored and special. When class was over, I couldn't wait to tell my mother what I'd seen. When I did, she smiled with satisfaction, knowing that God had used her skills to share his love.

Mother enjoyed that kind of giving throughout her life. One winter, when we lived in Ohio, a school bus broke down in front of our home. Mom invited all the students into our house for hot chocolate and cookies. Mom also liked to take home-baked goodies to the local fire station on holidays. Oddly, it was these paramedics who came to her aid when she was hit by a car.

❀ ❀ ❀

You Are His Hands

If you're like us, at times you find yourself in a rut. Day in and day out, life goes on in a monotonous pattern. If you're married, you greet your husband (if you can call it *greeting*) in the same tired tone of voice every afternoon. If you work, you go to your office with the same dull expression on your face day after day. When you call your friends, you can predict how the conversation will go because it's gone the same way so many times before.

In addition to being in a *life* rut, you can find yourself in a *friend-ship* rut. Your efforts to positively influence those around you seem to lack impact. It may be that your spiritual well is dry. God's living water—which literally sustains us and gives us life—is not bubbling up inside you, and therefore you have no overflow to pour out on your family and friends.

In order to share the love of Christ with others, we have to experience it first ourselves in a deep and tangible way. We must ask, "What kind of prayer life do I have?" "Do I read God's Word often?" "Am I turning away from those things in my life that I know to be sin?" "Am I surrounding myself with others who are like-minded when it comes to spiritual things?"

The answers to these questions are telling. Because you see, all of us are in one of three places in our lives. We may be experiencing a rich, fulfilling, life-impacting spiritual walk with God. Or we may be on the right track generally, but after pondering the previous questions, we realize we have a few areas that are deficient and need work. Or we may be in a third category: Our lives are definitely not impacting others with the joy, peace, and power that only God can bring, because we aren't living in friendship with God.

Having the God of the universe as a friend is an amazing thing. John 3:16 tells us, "For God so loved the world that he gave his one and only Son, that whoever believes in him shall not perish but have eternal life." If God gave the gift, then we must receive the gift in order to possess it. But what exactly does the gift include? Well, for one thing, it includes the promise of living with God forever after we die. But more than that, it includes the promise of his presence and his friendship in our daily lives.

How do we receive this incredible, life-changing gift? We receive it by believing that Jesus is God's perfect Son and by acknowledging that

In the same way, let your light shine before men, that they may see your good deeds and praise your Father in heaven.
—Matthew 5:16

in his death on the cross, he took on himself the punishment we deserve for living lives that aren't pleasing to him.

When we have a friendship with God—the kind of friendship that keeps us in constant communication with him—then we naturally desire to meet spiritual needs in the lives of our acquaintances, good friends, and of course, soul mates. Our eyes are opened to see creative ways in which we can spontaneously bless others in the daily routine of living. Blessing others without advanced planning becomes second nature!

But as wonderful as it is to be spontaneous, it's also important for us to take time out to think of ways to express the love of Christ to our friends. Here are some tangible, concrete ways to bless others that we've discovered over the years.

Write a Note of Encouragement

Determine to write one or two encouraging note cards to friends and loved ones every night, right before you turn off the light. Make it a habit. Keep cards or stationary, stamps, a pen, and your address book in a bedside table drawer. If your spouse has turned in early, use a book light to make your late-night correspondence courteous and convenient.

Take a Friend Along

When you decide to attend a spiritually uplifting event—say, a Christian concert or a ladies luncheon at your church—think of someone you could bless by taking her with you. If tickets are required in advance, buy two and ask the Lord who you should invite. Then call her and go!

Host a Bible Study

Open your home for a one-time event or a six- or eight-week

study. If you don't feel confident about leading the group, ask the Lord to direct you to another woman who could teach. There are many study resources available at local Christian bookstores. Choose a study based on the level of spiritual maturity of those you plan to invite.

Give Spiritually Encouraging Gifts

If you give birthday or Christmas gifts to your friends, consider purchasing Bibles, Christian books, spiritual journals, jewelry, or other items that carry a spiritual message. Gifts for "no reason" are always fun; so be on the lookout for meaningful gifts you can purchase or make, and have your eyes and your heart open to see who needs to receive them. Why not keep a few in your car—you just never know whom the Lord might place in your path as you go about your day.

Start a Prayer Chain

Ask several friends to be a part of a prayer chain. Create a list with everyone's name and phone number on it, then distribute the list to each participant. Tell your friends to call you whenever anything arises in their lives that requires prayer. When a call comes in, pray for the need, and then call the woman's name that is under yours to pass on the prayer concern. Each woman, in turn, prays and calls the next woman on the list.

These ideas are intended to get your own creativity jump-started. Add to this list as you come up with more creative ways to bless the friends God has placed in your life. Do you remember the words of that beloved old hymn "Let Others See Jesus in You," written by B. B. McKinney in 1922? The fourth verse so aptly summarizes the importance of sharing our faith with others: "Then live for Christ both day and night, be faithful, be brave, and true. And lead the lost to life and light; Let others see Jesus in you."[2] As positive friends, let's be sure our faith shines brightly through our words and actions in all of our relationships. We want our friends to see Jesus in us.

POWER POINT

⚙ **Read:** Acts 9:36–43, the story of Tabitha (also called Dorcas). What evidence do you see that this woman lived out her faith? How did she touch people's lives? In what ways are you like her?

🕊 **Pray:** Glorious Lord and Savior, thank you for giving your life for me, and thank you for filling my life with your love and warmth and peace. You are the light of my life! Shine brightly in all my words and actions so that your love through me can touch others. Open my eyes to see those who need to know you care, and show me ways to be a positive friend. Let my faith in you and my love for you be obvious to everyone I meet. In Jesus' name I pray, amen.

💡 **Remember:** "Let your light shine before men, that they may see your good deeds and praise your Father in heaven" (Matthew 5:16).

☺ **Do:** Ask yourself three questions: "Can others see the reality of my faith through my words and actions?" "Are there any changes I need to make in my life or any sins I need to turn from?" "What is one thing I can do today to live out my faith at home, at church, or in the community?" Take a step toward doing that one thing, and ask God to strengthen and guide you in the process.

Dorcas – used the gifts that God gave her to the best of her ability. Everyone she touched remembered + loved her —

Power Principle #6

THe
P**o**wer
oF
h**o**nesty

Honesty means integrity in everything. Honesty means wholeness, completeness; it means truth in everything—in deed and in word.

—Orison Swett Marden

For we can do nothing against the truth, but only for the truth.

—2 Corinthians 13:8 NASB

Confronting with Love
The Importance of Accountability and Openness

It is the best and truest friend who honestly tells us the truth about ourselves even when he knows we shall not like it. False friends are the ones who hide such truth from us and do so in order to remain in our favor.

—R. C. H. Lenski

Michelle and Trisha met seven years ago when Trisha moved into Michelle's neighborhood. Michelle showed up on Trisha's doorstep with a smile on her face and fresh-baked cookies in hand. Through the clutter of unpacked boxes, Trisha maneuvered Michelle to a cozy place on the sofa, and their friendship began. They had so much in common. Their children were about the same ages. They both worked part time. They were each involved in church activities. Their husbands were self-employed. Best of all, their personalities really clicked.

It was summertime, and these new friends spent hours laughing and sharing with each other as they watched their children swim or swing at the park. In only a few short months, a deep and heartfelt friendship was established. Then school kicked into full gear, and their busy family schedules meant they couldn't see each other nearly as much. Still their quick visits together were always meaningful and enjoyable.

That fall Michelle's husband, Bill, began spending significant

Therefore each of you must put off falsehood and speak truthfully to his neighbor, for we are all members of one body. —Ephesians 4:25

amounts of work-related time out of town. Michelle was left with her hands full as she tried to manage her children, her job, and the ongoing renovations on her house without much help. Over time Trisha noticed that her friend was no longer her usual joyful self. The high energy and zeal for life that so characterized Michelle had been replaced by discontentment and exhaustion.

Trisha also noticed that Bill's trips were getting longer and longer— and Michelle was mentioning him in conversation less and less. And she couldn't help but notice one other thing: Michelle had struck up an unusually friendly relationship with the man who was doing the renovations on her house. Almost every time Trisha looked out her front window, she saw the contractor's car in Michelle's driveway, sometimes late into the night.

Trisha was heartsick. She knew that Michelle, deep in her heart, believed in the truths found in God's Word. She knew that her friend believed in God's plan for marriage. She knew that she was committed to her family. So Trisha prayed and then loved Michelle enough to confront her with her concerns.

With tears running down her cheeks, Trisha asked Michelle about her late-night visitor. Michelle, feeling no condemnation from her friend, poured out her pain, hurt and loneliness from the depths of her being. She confided to Trisha that the "new man" in her life made her feel special and appreciated—but he was only a "good friend." He held her hand and held her close, nothing more.

But that explanation didn't satisfy Trisha. Lovingly but boldly she pointed out to her friend that she was playing with fire. She encouraged Michelle to slam the door on temptation and cling to the comfort that only the Lord can give to a lonely and hurting heart. Her words were hard, but her heart toward Michelle was soft. Trisha valued their friendship so much that she was willing to risk their relationship in order to do what was best for her friend.

It's Not Easy—but It's Necessary

Can you remember your mother or father saying, right before they disciplined you, "This is going to hurt me more than it hurts you"? Both of us swore we would never say that to our own children. And you know what? We can't count the number of times we have used those exact words with our kids before we applied loving discipline.

When it comes to our relationships, we'd all rather be cheerleaders than corrections officers. But if we truly love people, we want what's best for them—and sometimes that "best" requires confrontation and discipline. You've heard the saying "It's a tough job, but somebody has to do it!" As positive friends, we need to be that "somebody."

Jesus was a master at confronting people. He did not shy away from telling it like it was. Many times in Scripture he demonstrated that godly correction has the power to transform one life and potentially many more through its ripple effect.

John 4 tells the story of Jesus, a Jew, befriending a woman from Samaria. According to the social norms of that day, this woman had several strikes against her. First, she was a woman, which meant she had little social standing. Second, she was a Samaritan, which made her "unclean" and inferior in the eyes of the Jews. Her third strike was something that caused her to be despised not only by the Jews, but also by her own people—even the other Samaritan women: She was immoral.

None of these strikes phased Jesus in the least. He had been traveling and had stopped to rest by a well. The Bible tells us, "When a Samaritan woman came to draw water, Jesus said to her, 'Will you give me a drink?' (His disciples had gone into the town to buy food.) The Samaritan woman said to him, 'You are a Jew and I am a Samaritan woman. How can you ask me for a drink?'" (John 4:7–9).

Jesus proceeded to tell this woman about God's gift of living water that would satisfy her spiritual thirst. "Sir, give me this water so that I won't get thirsty and have to keep coming here to draw water," she said in verse 15. That's when an amazing thing happened. Jesus responded to her request by first addressing the sin in her life.

He told her to go and get her husband. When she replied that she had no husband, Jesus said to her, "You are right when you say you have no husband. The fact is, you have had five husbands, and the man you now have is not your husband. What you have just said is quite true" (John 4:17–18).

This gal at the well must have been amazed. This man of God— who, it was beginning to dawn on her, *was* God—loved her despite her lack of morality and social pedigree. He cared enough to confront her sin while upholding her value and dignity. Note that Jesus confronted her while the disciples were away. He did not publicly humiliate her; instead, he privately addressed her spiritual neediness.

When the disciples arrived, the woman went back to her town and told the people, "Come, see a man who told me everything I ever did. Could this be the Christ?" (v. 29). She didn't try to repeat all that he had said to her. After all, it wasn't lofty philosophizing that so deeply affected her; it was the fact that Jesus loved her even though he knew her dark, ugly secrets. His gentle but direct confrontation led to a transformed life. And her life was not the only life revolutionized that day. Many people in her village, after seeing the change in her life, wanted to meet the Master for themselves.

Conviction, Not Condemnation

When God directs a confrontation, the result is conviction, not condemnation. Consider Anne's story. Anne was a senior at a Midwestern university. On one particular evening, she found herself in an unusual position: alone. Her three roommates had not yet returned to the apartment from their day's activities. So Anne decided to take advantage of the solitude by kneeling beside their couch to pray.

No sooner had she entered into her dialogue with God, however, than she felt strongly impressed to pray for a fellow student named Chad. Anne and Chad had entered the university together as freshmen and had become good friends. Chad was one of those guys who had it all. He was handsome, athletic, and smart, with just the right amount of cockiness to be appealing. He was a born leader, and people were instantly drawn to his charismatic charm. His high school accomplishments and activities were many, including being president of his school's Fellowship of Christian Athletes chapter.

When he started college, he had an obvious commitment to God. But as his freshman year rolled into his sophomore, junior, and then senior years, something changed. Yes, he was still handsome, athletic, smart, and a natural leader. He was the social chairman and then the president of his popular fraternity. But something was missing. His zeal for Christ had gotten lost along the way.

As Anne began to pray fervently that night that Chad would return to God, she began to weep. Scripture after scripture came to her mind that addressed the sinful choices he was making in his life. She strongly sensed that the Lord wanted her to confront him with the truth of God's Word. But she continued to labor in prayer, telling God all the reasons why she couldn't possibly confront her friend. The Lord was

An honest man is the noblest work of God. —Alexander Pope

☺

217

persistent, however. So despite the fact that it was getting late, Anne drove to Chad's apartment, a Bible in her hand and a heavy burden on her heart.

When Chad opened the door, he was obviously surprised to see her. Their friendship was not as strong as it had been in previous years.

"I drove over here to show you something I have in my car," Anne said.

He followed her to the car, and they both got in. That's when he saw tears streaming from his friend's eyes. Anne picked up her Bible and began to read to him the Scripture verses concerning his sin. She encouraged him to lay his gifts of physical attractiveness, intelligence, and leadership at the throne of God. She pleaded with him to return to righteous living.

Chad was speechless. Anne's pointed words deeply penetrated his heart and mind. He listened because he could sense her loving care for him.

When Anne left Chad that night, she didn't know what his response would be to her tearful message. All she knew was that she had been obedient to God. Then, several weeks before graduation, a letter came. As Anne read Chad's words, her heart sang:

Dear Anne,

You will never know what an impact you have made in my life. What you were willing to do stands out in my mind as one of the finest things anyone has ever done for me. Thank you for your boldness and your concern for me. I didn't want us to go our separate ways without you knowing that I have returned to the Lord.

Sincerely,
Chad

Why wasn't Chad offended by Anne's strong words of reprimand? Why was he willing to listen? Because he never felt condemned. *Condemnation* leads to despair and hopelessness, which can lead to anger, resentment, and denial. *Conviction,* on the other hand, leads to remorse, repentance, restoration, and renewal. There's a big difference! When we're willing to obey God by confronting and correcting someone we care about, we become a tool in God's hands to bring conviction, not condemnation. We become part of his plan of redemption for the one we love.

The Tools of Loving Confrontation

When it comes to confrontation, approach is everything. We often tell our teenagers, "It's not what you say but how you say it." They don't seem to get it quite yet, but they will! As adults we have a better understanding of how important it is to say hard things in a tender, caring way. We know from experience that the package containing the delicate and breakable contents of a person's heart is marked *Fragile.* We must handle it with care.

When you sense that God is prompting you to confront a friend or loved one, do it lovingly, using the following five tools:

The Tool of Self-Appraisal

You've probably heard people say that they don't go to church because the church is full of hypocrites. Well, they're right. Every church is filled with people like us—people who believe in their hearts and profess with their mouths one thing and then, every once in a while, turn around and do something completely contradictory. It's called sin. And of course, all of us sin. What makes matters worse is that we often fail to repent, yet we waste no time pointing out the faults of others.

If we're going to be used by God to help restore a friend who is making harmful decisions, we must first take a long, hard look at our own lives. We can't effectively confront a friend about a "wrong" they have committed against us without first asking God to search our hearts and reveal the sin that lies deep within us.

Psalm 139:23–24 states, "Search me, O God, and know my heart; test me and know my anxious thoughts. See if there is any offensive way in me, and lead me in the way everlasting." Yes, our loving Father is the one who judges our motives and our actions. But we're mistaken if we think we're not supposed to discern our own wrong actions and behavior. Clearly we are to use discernment based on how our behavior lines up with God's Word.

Before we go around pointing out the sinful actions of others, we must first heed Jesus' instruction in Luke 6:39–42:

> Can a blind man lead a blind man? Will they not both fall into a pit? A student is not above his teacher, but everyone who is fully trained will be like his teacher.
>
> Why do you look at the speck of sawdust in your brother's eye and pay no attention to the plank in your own eye? How can you say to your brother, "Brother, let me take the speck out of your eye," when you yourself fail to see the plank in your own eye? You hypocrite, first take the plank out of your eye, and then you will see clearly to remove the speck from your brother's eye.

Terry Ann reflects: We can be so quick to judge! Just recently I overheard a woman in our church criticizing the way a few of the girls in the youth group were dressing. Now I freely admit, I agreed with her contention that low-rise jeans, midriff-bearing crop tops, and skin-tight, low-cut T-shirts are inappropriate and violate God's instruction concerning modesty. However, the woman making the complaint was dressed in an extremely form-fitting dress that shouted to the world, "Look at my figure." If she had confronted the girls that day regarding their lack of modesty, her accurate rebuke would have fallen on deaf ears!

❖ ❖ ❖

It's no wonder that teenagers—and many of the rest of us—are confused. Often we say, in essence, "Do as I say, not as I do!" We must use the tool of self-appraisal to check our own motives, actions, and attitudes before we attempt to instruct a friend (or anyone else, for that matter) on how to live.

The Tool of Humility

Carolyn and Jan had known each other for years. Although they had never spent much time socializing, they had been continuously involved in each other's lives as they served on various church committees together and taught one another's children in Sunday school. Each woman knew that the other had a desire to live in a way that pleased God.

Over a period of time, however, Carolyn began to notice that Jan wasn't as friendly as she once was. But life was busy, and she let the matter go for several months. She was probably reading too much into Jan's lack of warmth anyway, she figured.

Then one Sunday morning, Jan completely disregarded Carolyn's friendly greeting. Stunned and puzzled, Carolyn knew she must confront her friend. After Sunday school, she pulled Jan aside and said with true remorse, "Jan, I feel certain I have done something that has offended you. I've thought and thought, and honestly I don't know what it is. But I have missed the bond we used to share. Please tell me why you have pulled back on our friendship."

The ice was finally broken. Jan hesitated at first, but then she began to talk about the problem. Several months earlier she'd heard that Carolyn had instigated a petition to oust one of the church leaders—a man who was a close friend of Jan's husband. Carolyn was shocked. The report was totally false! She explained to Jan that she didn't start the petition or sign the petition; in fact, she'd never even seen it. Whoever was passing it around knew better than to bring it to her!

What a load was lifted from the hearts of these two women who desired to be in right relationship with God and with others! Carolyn's willingness to humbly approach her friend led to a restored friendship.

Notice that Carolyn first looked within herself to see what she might have done to offend Jan. Humility allowed her to assume that one of two things had happened: Either she had unintentionally caused the tension between them, or there had been a misunderstanding.

The dictionary defines *humility* this way: "A modest opinion of one's own importance or rank."[1] Correction, when dosed out with an air of superiority, is a hard pill to swallow. No one likes a know-it-all. However, when we are willing to humble ourselves, admitting our weaknesses and mistakes, then we're no longer a threat to others. Humility has a way of defusing a confrontational situation. It allows the person we are confronting to feel accepted and even appreciated.

God values humility. In Luke 18 Jesus taught a lesson on humility to a group of religious leaders who needed a strong dose of that particular virtue. Interestingly, he used the indirect approach of storytelling to confront these leaders about their self-righteous behavior. Jesus was an expert in the area of confrontation! His approach always differed depending on the situation and the people involved. Here's the story he told:

Two men went up to the temple to pray, one a Pharisee and the other a tax collector. The Pharisee stood up and prayed about himself: "God, I thank you that I am not like other men—robbers, evildoers, adulterers—or even like this tax collector. I fast twice a week and give a tenth of all I get."

But the tax collector stood at a distance. He would not even look up to heaven, but beat his breast and said, "God, have mercy on me, a sinner."

I tell you that this man, rather than the other, went home justified before God. For everyone who exalts himself will be humbled, and he who humbles himself will be exalted. (Luke 18:10–14)

We must be like the tax collector. We must recognize that nothing we do in and of ourselves is of any value; our entire self-worth is based on God's work in us. This acknowledgment causes us to be humble. We refuse to take a lofty position and look down our noses at others. We confront and correct those we care about out of obedience to God— not from a sense of superiority, but rather from a sense that we, too, are sinners in need of God's grace. When our hearts are humble, everything that we have to say is a lot more palatable. Never confront without a humble heart!

The Tool of Prayer

Prayer is an important tool to use before confrontation because it makes our hearts right. It enables us to discern truth in a situation. It's the avenue through which we get our direction from God.

We don't want to simply talk about prayer; we must immerse ourselves in it. Remember, it was during Anne's time alone with God that God impressed on her heart the need to confront her friend Chad. No one can say that her meeting with Chad was anything but a God-thing. We are reminded in James 1:5 to ask for wisdom, and God will give it to us generously. Clearly, God gave Anne the wisdom that she needed.

We need to pray for wisdom not only in what to say, but in how to say it: "Lord, guide my tongue. Lead me by your truth to say the right thing in the right way."

We also need to pray for God to prepare the listener's heart. If we were gardeners, we would want to plant our seeds in fertile soil, wouldn't we? Since our intent in confrontation is to bring seeds of truth to a person's heart, we must pray for that heart to be open and ready to receive: "Lord, give my friend ears to hear and a heart to understand." Our job is the delivery, yes; but it is also to pray for the reception. That includes praying for God's direction about the right time and place to speak so that we have the best chance of being heard. Jesus knew, for example, that when he met the Samaritan woman alone at the well, the time and place was right for her to hear the truth about her life.

The Tool of God's Truth

Second Timothy 3:16–17 tells us, "All Scripture is God-breathed and is useful for teaching, rebuking, correcting and training in righteousness, so that the man of God may be thoroughly equipped for every good work." The Bible must be our baseline when we are considering a confrontation of any sort, especially when the person we're confronting is a believer in Christ. Christians may have different viewpoints and opinions on matters ranging from drinking to hair length to managing money. It's not our place to impose our viewpoints on others. When it comes to foundational scriptural principles, however, we have grounds for confrontation, as Trisha did when she confronted Michelle in the story at the beginning of this chapter.

The Bible is not only a plumb line for knowing what issues are worth confronting, it's also a tool we can use in the process. God's Word speaks to the heart of a believer in a powerful way. Hebrews 4:12 says, "For the word of God is living and active. Sharper than any double-edged sword, it penetrates even to dividing soul and spirit, joints and marrow; it judges the thoughts and attitudes of the heart." Sharing Scripture is a powerful and effective way to confront a believer who is caught in sin. We don't have the power to change another person, but God's Spirit working through God's Word does.

Perhaps you're wondering, *What about non-Christian friends? Are we supposed to judge them in the same way we do Christian friends and hold them accountable to God's Word?* Paul addressed this matter with the early Corinthian church. The situation at the church was detestable! Not only were the Corinthians allowing a man who was sleeping with his father's wife to be a part of their fellowship, they were bragging about it! Paul confronted them, telling them that their boasting was not good and that they needed to boot the immoral Christian out of the church so that "the sinful nature may be destroyed and his spirit saved on the day of the Lord" (1 Corinthians 5:5).

Paul went on to say in verses 9–13:

> I have written you in my letter not to associate with sexually immoral people—not at all meaning the people of this world who are immoral, or the greedy and swindlers, or idolaters. In that case you would have to leave this world. But now I am writing you that you must not associate with anyone who calls himself a brother but is sexually immoral or greedy, an idolater or a slanderer, a drunkard or a swindler. With such a man do not even eat.
>
> What business is it of mine to judge those outside the church? Are you not to judge those inside? God will judge those outside. "Expel the wicked man from among you."

Clearly, it is not our job to confront non-Christian friends on the grounds of biblical standards. We can offer advice and wisdom to help them see the benefit of living according to God's principles. But biblical confrontation is reserved for believers, since they fall under the authority of Scripture.

We're not saying that we shouldn't share the Word with unbelievers. The Word of God is powerful and can touch even the coldest hearts. Frank M. Goodchild tells a story about a learned Chinese man who was employed by missionaries to translate the New Testament into a certain Chinese dialect. At first the translating effort made little difference to the scholarly Chinese man; but after a while he was moved to exclaim, "What a wonderful book this is!" When the missionary asked why, the man replied, "Because it tells so exactly about myself. It knows all that is in me. The One who made this book must have made me!"[2]

The Tool of Praise

Actress Julie Andrews gave a truly delightful performance when she portrayed the strong-willed but lovingly creative nanny in the movie *Mary Poppins.* Our parents must have taken us to see that film at least a half-dozen times when it came out in the 1960s! One of the most memorable tunes that Mary Poppins sang went like this: "Just a spoonful of sugar helps the medicine go down…"

Correction is to the spiritually sick heart what medication is to the physically sick body. But correction and medication are both hard to swallow at times. That's where the tool of praise comes in. Praise is the sugar that helps the medicine of correction go down. In order for us to respond positively to correction, we must first feel appreciated and accepted by the one who is dosing out the rebuke. A positive word really helps! As Dale Carnegie says in his classic book *How to Win Friends and Influence People,* "Beginning with praise is like the dentist who begins his work with Novocain. The patient still gets a drilling, but the Novocain is pain-killing."[3]

Abraham Lincoln did a masterful job of using praise before giving a strong word of correction in a letter he penned to General Joseph Hooker on April 26, 1863, during a grave period of the Civil War. The Union Army met with defeat after defeat. Morale was low, and even Lincoln was at the point of despair. He felt it was imperative to write to General Hooker and point out certain errors that were affecting the conduct of the war. Note how diplomatic but firm Lincoln was in his approach:

> I have placed you at the head of the Army of the Potomac. Of course, I have done this upon what appears to me to be sufficient reasons, and yet I think it best for you to know that there are some things in regard to which I am not quite satisfied with you.
>
> I believe you to be a brave and skillful soldier, which, of course, I like. I also believe you do not mix politics with your profession, in which you are right. You have confidence in yourself, which is a valuable if not an indispensable quality.
>
> You are ambitious, which, within reasonable bounds, does good rather than harm. But I think that during General Burnside's command of the army you have taken counsel of your ambition and thwarted him as much as you could, in which you did a great wrong to the country and to a most meritorious and honorable brother officer.
>
> I have heard, in such a way as to believe it, of your recently saying that both the army and the Government needed a dictator. Of course, it was not for this, but in spite of it, that I have given you command.
>
> Only those generals who gain successes can set up as dictators. What I now ask of you is military success, and I will risk the dictatorship.

The Government will support you to the utmost of its ability, which is neither more nor less than it has done and will do for all commanders. I much fear that the spirit, which you have aided to infuse into the army, of criticizing their commander and withholding confidence from him, will now turn upon you. I shall assist you, as far as I can, to put it down.

Neither you nor Napoleon, if he were alive again, could get any good out of an army while such spirit prevails in it, and now beware of rashness. Beware of rashness, but with energy and sleepless vigilance go forward and give us victories.[4]

Even though Lincoln corrected Hooker, he did so while also praising the general for his many attributes. Apparently our sixteenth president knew the value of a spoonful of sugar!

The Best Approach

Lincoln's example brings up a point: There are a variety of modes of communication that we can use to confront someone. We believe that whenever possible, face-to-face confrontation is best. We might invite the person to our home or out to lunch or coffee so that we can talk privately. Other times a letter can be an appropriate and gentle way to express our concerns. By putting our thoughts in writing, we can make sure we're expressing ourselves accurately and with the right tone. We also create a written account that can be referred back to as often as necessary. Just remember, a letter continues to exist long after an issue is resolved. In some cases, that may be a good thing; in others, maybe not.

Choose your form of communication carefully! A phone call can be good in certain situations; but then we miss facial expressions, which can tell us so much. We need to pray and ask God to lead us to the best approach.

One thing we should never do: Have our concerns delivered second-hand. We've all seen couples—television sitcoms get a lot of mileage from them—who refuse to talk to each other, so they pass messages back and forth through their children. "Go tell your father…" "Go tell your mother…" Nothing ever gets resolved that way! If we have a message that we want delivered to a friend, then we must love and care for that friend enough to deliver the message ourselves. Confrontation may be done through a variety of methods, but if we're going to be positive friends, it must be done directly.

Putting Excuses Aside

Why is it that we don't want to confront others, even when we know God has called us to do it? As we said earlier, it's a tough job. Confrontation is awkward and uncomfortable. It's so much easier to ignore a wrongdoing and leave well enough alone. Besides, if we confront a friend, our relationship could change—and not necessarily for the better.

Whatever our excuses, we have to put them aside. Matthew 18:15–17 is clear about what we must do:

> If your brother sins against you [some manuscripts do not have the words, *against you*] go and show him his fault, just between the two of you. If he listens to you, you have won your brother over. But if he will not listen, take one or two others along, so that "every matter may be established by the testimony of two or three witnesses." If he refuses to listen to them, tell it to the church; and if he refuses to listen even to the church, treat him as you would a pagan or a tax collector.

If the person being confronted receives the correction and repents, then the relationship can be restored. But the offender makes the choice. If you have approached your friend with a heart truly motivated by love, yet you find that your pleas for repentance are met with disdain or denial, then its time to move on. You've done your part. You can do no more except continue to pray that your friend will one day choose righteousness. Even Jesus encouraged his disciples to go into a town, present the truth of God's message of salvation, and if their words were not received, wipe the dust from their feet and go on to the next place (see Matthew 10:14).

We must love God enough to obey his command to confront one another in love. And we must love our friends enough to confront them even if it means the friendship may be sacrificed.

Positive friends are not on a continual lookout for opportunities to confront each other. In fact, we're called to love our friends through many faults. But when a situation arises and you know that God is directing you to confront a friend, do it in his strength, wisdom, and integrity. Use the tools we've described in this chapter. Only fools rush into controversy; wise friends lovingly and prayerfully confront.

POWER POINT

🌸 **Read:** Ephesians 5:1–21. What principles for confrontation can you glean from this passage? Make a verse-by-verse list of the principles you see.

♡ **Pray:** Glorious Lord, I am so grateful for your unfailing love. I praise you for sending your Son to die for my sins and to rise again, giving me eternal hope. Examine my life and convict me of my wicked ways. Lead me in the way everlasting. Oh Lord, I want to be so careful when it comes to confrontation! Guide and direct me, and help me to say and do only what is in your will. Show me clearly when it is time to confront someone, and give me the wisdom to do it with your Word and in your grace. In Jesus' name, amen.

💡 **Remember:** "Be very careful, then, how you live—not as unwise but as wise, making the most of every opportunity, because the days are evil" (Ephesians 5:15–16).

😊 **Do:** What is your attitude toward confrontation? Are you open to giving correction if necessary? More importantly, are you willing to receive it? Is there a friend on your heart whom you know the Lord wants you to confront (for a biblically based reason)? If so, be obedient, follow the steps in this chapter, and go forward in God's power and grace.

① Be imitators of God - beloved Children
walk in love
obscenity - coarse joking

15

Masks We Wear
Being Real with Your Friends

To thine own self be true, and it must follow, as the night the day,
thou canst not then be false to any man.

—William Shakespeare

Trying to keep up a certain image can wear a person out. Take Nadia for instance. She always prided herself on her talent for entertaining. Although she verbally denied it with a humble, "Oh, I only wish!" she actually loved it when people compared her to Martha Stewart. Each season she hosted a ladies luncheon at her home, serving recipes directly out of *Gourmet Magazine* and decorating the house to the hilt in the appropriate seasonal style. She worked for weeks to prepare for her next event. Her family learned that it was best not to bug Mom with needs or requests on the week of her luncheon.

Nadia competed with herself, always trying to outdo her previous effort. Table favors, centerpieces, and dessert truffles became almost an obsession as she worked to keep up her "hostess of the year" image. One particular Christmas nearly did her in. The day before the luncheon, her daughter came down with the flu. This was the day Nadia had planned to shop for flowers, favors, and attend to final details—and now it was blown on a child who needed her nose blown.

Nadia made sure everyone in the family knew how inconvenient this flu was for her. She was frazzled, even angry, knowing that her luncheon was not going to be the picture-perfect event it had been in the past. Her daughter had better be well by the next day, because she couldn't cook and have all those guests show up while a sick child was in the next room demanding her attention.

The day of the luncheon Nadia's daughter was better—sort of—so she wrapped her up, gave her some cough medicine, and sent her off to school. *There,* she thought. *At least now I can make the final preparations for my Swiss cheese puffs and tomato-basil cream soup.*

As she was busily cooking and quietly fretting over not having the cute favors she'd wanted to provide, the phone rang. It was the school. Her daughter needed to come home. She still had a fever, and she felt awful.

No! Nadia thought. *I don't have time for this!*

All the way home in the car, Nadia expressed her frustration and worry about how this party was going to be her worst ever. All her daughter could do was utter a meek "I'm sorry."

When they pulled into the driveway, Nadia told her daughter to go get into bed. Then she rushed into the house, finished a few more cheese puffs, lit some candles, and began greeting guests at the door. She wore a fake smile (well, it was more of a smirk) as she said hello. When people complimented her on another fantastic luncheon, she lied, "It was nothing really."

We all can relate in some small way to Nadia. Each of us has had the experience of putting up a front to cover the way we're really feeling or thinking. To some extent we all wear masks. That's not necessarily a bad thing. A mask can be healthy—a natural and prudent piece of protective gear. After all, we simply cannot share all and bare all with every person we meet. We need to be discerning about whom we share the nitty-gritty details of our lives with, because not everyone can be trusted. If we let every person we meet know everything there is to know about us, we'd probably end up with very few friends, and our life stories would be splattered everywhere by ruthless gossips.

Jesus warned his followers in Matthew 7:6, "Do not give dogs what is sacred; do not throw your pearls to pigs. If you do, they may trample them under their feet, and then turn and tear you to pieces." We are not being fake when we choose to use discernment in deciding how much we share with others. We are simply guarding our lives and the lives of our families from unnecessary harm.

A mask is unhealthy, however, when it's used to always present and maintain a certain image that we want the world to see. We think, *I can't let anyone know what I'm really like, so I will put on this costume, this facade, this front, so people will think I'm better than I really am.* A mask of this nature prevents us from getting close to others, because we can't be honest or real. The common bonds of friendship are always built on truth and honesty. We can't be positive friends and wear masks at the same time.

The Great Pretenders

The word *hypocrite* originally referred to Greek actors on the stage. Because Greek plays required men to play a variety of roles, the actors used masks to hide their real identities and to present the images they wanted the audience to see. Over time *hypocrite* has grown to become a term people use to identify a pretender—someone who pretends to be something he or she is not. It specifically refers to making a false pretense or putting up an image that gives people the idea that you are one thing when, in fact, you are quite another.

Jesus used the word *hypocrite* to identify the Pharisees—religious leaders who put on a show of being very pious and devoted to God when in fact they were jealous liars and deceivers. Let's take a look at what Jesus had to say to these Pharisees in Matthew 23:13–15, 23–28. Warning: You're about to hear Jesus really put it to them! His strong words make plain his disgust with fake exteriors:

> You shut the kingdom of heaven in men's faces. You yourselves do not enter, nor will you let those enter who are trying to.
>
> Woe to you, teachers of the law and Pharisees, you hypocrites! You travel over land and sea to win a single convert, and when he becomes one, you make him twice as much a son of hell as you are.…
>
> Woe to you, teachers of the law and Pharisees, you hypocrites! You give a tenth of your spices—mint, dill and cumin. But you have neglected the more important matters of the law—justice, mercy and faithfulness. You should have practiced the latter, without neglecting the former. You blind guides! You strain out a gnat but swallow a camel.
>
> Woe to you, teachers of the law and Pharisees, you hypocrites! You clean the outside of the cup and dish, but inside they are full of greed and self-indulgence. Blind Pharisee! First clean the inside of the cup and dish, and then the outside also will be clean.
>
> Woe to you, teachers of the law and Pharisees, you hypocrites! You are like whitewashed tombs, which look beautiful on the outside but on the inside are full of dead men's bones and everything unclean. In the same way, on the outside you appear to people as righteous but on the inside you are full of hypocrisy and wickedness.

Whoa! Jesus really let these guys have it! But then, what could be said about us? Is the image we're presenting on the outside a truthful portrayal of what's going on inside? Jesus' words are a wake-up call for each of us to consider our own hypocrisy. We need to ask ourselves, "Is there any double standard in me? Are there masks that need to be dismantled?" Let's be honest. We all need a little cleaning up on the inside. Each of us needs to have our hearts and minds continually purified through Christ and the work of the Holy Spirit in our lives. Then as we become clean on the inside, that purity will be automatically reflected on the outside.

We need to keep our focus on our own hearts, not the hearts of others. Only God knows what's in someone else's heart. We don't. Certainly, Jesus knew what was in the hearts and minds of the Pharisees when he called them on the carpet. That's why he was able to do so! We can't be as quick to judge, however, because we don't always know how another person's inside matches up with the outside. Many times we can be very wrong.

❦

Karol reflects: Case in point: Terry Ann and I both have sanguine personalities. Both of us tend to be a little more bright and cheery than others. Some may even think we're a little over the top! We love to be around people, and it shows. At times, however, our genuineness has been questioned by people who assume our cheeriness must be fake. (Our next chapter will deal with the danger of assumptions, by the way.) Of course, we both need to constantly examine ourselves to make sure our outsides and our insides are matching. But the good news is, neither one of us hesitates to cry and weep with people when we are sad or to get angry when we are frustrated. We don't put on our "cheery masks" when our emotions are anything but cheery!

We're not saying that we are perfectly genuine in every way. We are simply pointing out that it is easy to make assumptions about others.

❀ ❀ ❀

The Hall of Masks

The difficult thing about a mask is that we often don't recognize that we've put it on! Let's take a brief look at some of the most common masks women tend to wear in their lives. This overview may help each of us detect our own favorite *faux* facades.

Everything's Perfect mask: Some people don't want to let their guard down even for a moment. They wear a mask that says everything in their lives is just fine. They don't want anyone to see that they have a weakness or a problem. Sometimes it's a matter of pride; sometimes they're afraid that if they are honest about their hurts, they will be a burden to others.

Perfectly in Control mask: This is the mask worn by many control freaks—not only for their own security, but also to demonstrate to others that they have everything organized and under control.

Poor Pitiful Me mask: Many a melancholy soul wears this picture of pitifulness. "Everything is wrong and you should feel sorry for me" is this person's continuous tune.

Elitist Snob mask: This is the "I'm better than you" mask. Whether people present themselves as superior in wealth or cars or clothes or grades or beauty, they put on the cover of snobbery.

Humble Pie mask: Oddly enough, this mask is rooted in self-centeredness, although it doesn't appear that way at first. False humility creeps in on well-intentioned people as they pretend not to accept credit or glory. But the truth is, they are soaking up the praise on the inside while trying to look humble on the outside. Almost everyone is guilty of donning this mask at one time or another. True humility is a gift from God.

Supermom mask: In our society, the pressure is on to be the best mom by raising the cutest, most perfect kids (with the highest grades); volunteering at school for every field trip; and shuttling budding athletes, artists, and musicians to every possible practice, game, or lesson. Certainly no mom wants to be second-rate, so many women put on this mask to maintain the supermom image.

Perfect Homemaker mask: It's easy to get caught in the House Beautiful syndrome. People who put on this mask are out to earn the Good Housekeeping Award for neatness and décor. The perfect homemaker couldn't or wouldn't want anyone to think she has messy piles of clutter to contend with (like everyone else does)!

Holy and Religious mask: That pious mask can look so good—perfect church attendance, membership on the hospitality and stewardship committees, leadership council for women's Bible study, and so on. Unfortunately women who wear this mask have a tendency to look down their noses at everyone else's sin, thankfully certain that they would never participate in such a thing!

I Can Do It All mask: Our culture offers us a myriad of opportunities. That's a good thing. But some women want to show the world that they can have a career, be active in volunteering, raise a family, take a class, and run a marathon, all at the same time. Yes, they can juggle it all—or if they can't, they'll wear a mask that says they can!

I Can't Do Anything mask: The flip side is the woman who whines in despair, "I can't do anything." Deep inside she knows she is as capable as anyone. But she's afraid to try, so she puts on a mask and tells herself (and everyone else) that she doesn't have the ability.

Self-Confidence mask: This facade gives the impression that the wearer is totally self-assured. She can conquer the world! But many

For by the grace given me I say to every one of you: do not think of yourself more highly than you ought, but rather think of yourself with sober judgment, in accordance with the measure of faith God has given you. —Romans 12:3

☺

239

women who present this image are actually fearful inside, afraid that someone will find the chinks in their armor.

Bitter Betty mask: When a woman puts on this sour, scowling cover, she lets the world know that she has been hurt, and she's not about to let it go or move on. Besides, it's someone else's fault that she's this way—at least, that's her story, and she's sticking to it!

Best Performance mask: The person who wears this mask believes that whatever she does, she must do it better than anyone else. Whether it is playing in the tennis league, selling candy bars for the fundraiser, or organizing the office Christmas party, people must see that she is the best. Unfortunately, staying on this performance track is quite tiring and leaves innocent lives in the wake.

Did you recognize a favorite mask or two? Certainly, we could add many more to the list. Most of us do not simply wear one mask; we wear many over a lifetime. We rarely put them on deliberately, of course. They go up almost by reflex. Sometimes, if we become aware of a particular mask, we can learn to break away from it; but if we're not watchful, a new one can easily take its place.

Why Masks?

Pride and insecurity seem to be at the root of most masks. We may not recognize pride at first; it tends to set up its insidious kingdom in our hearts and minds by pretending to be something else, like humility, service, or even responsibility. Often pride and insecurity develop within us because we've taken our eyes off of God and his loving plan for our lives and put them on others who seem to be doing "better" than us.

In Psalm 73:1–9 we see a description of people who wear masks. Notice that the psalmist almost stumbled with envy as he observed the prideful masqueraders:

Surely God is good to Israel,
> to those who are pure in heart.

But as for me, my feet had almost slipped;
> I had nearly lost my foothold.

For I envied the arrogant
> when I saw the prosperity of the wicked.

They have no struggles;
> their bodies are healthy and strong.

They are free from the burdens common to man;
> they are not plagued by human ills.

Therefore pride is their necklace;
> they clothe themselves with violence.

From their callous hearts comes iniquity;
> the evil conceits of their minds know no limits.

They scoff, and speak with malice;
> in their arrogance they threaten oppression.

Their mouths lay claim to heaven,
> and their tongues take possession of the earth.

The people being described by the psalmist are the kind who want everyone to think that they have it all together, that their lives are perfect. How easy it is for us to want people to think we are perfect! Did you notice in this passage that pride is the necklace of those who give the my-life-is-perfect image? The psalmist goes on to describe the way prideful people usually end up: "Surely you [God] place them on slippery ground; you cast them down to ruin. How suddenly are they destroyed, completely swept away by terrors!" (vv. 18–19).

We're on slippery ground when we try to wear a mask or maintain a facade. The house of cards will eventually fall down. No one can maintain a perfect image forever.

Psalm 73 continues with the call of a person with a pure heart—a person who looks to God alone for identity, security, and strength. Oh, if only we could all drop our prideful masks and say with the psalmist, "Whom have I in heaven but you? And earth has nothing I desire besides you. My flesh and my heart may fail, but God is the strength of my heart and my portion forever" (vv. 25–26).

✿

Terry Ann reflects: I'm reminded of a time in college when I felt I shouldn't let even my roommates see when I was emotionally hurt or discouraged. I wore the "Everything's Perfect" mask. While I was always available to help other people through their troubles, no one ever knew when I was struggling with anything. I maintained a "together" image all the time, even with close Christian friends.

One quiet evening my roommate Julie and I were studying alone in our apartment. Since our other roommates were out, Julie decided this was a good opportunity to talk to me and express some concerns.

"Terry Ann, none of us feel that we can get close to you," Julie said. "You never let us see your downside. What are your needs or challenges or failings? We need to know."

It was a watershed moment for me. I had always kept my guard up, thinking that if anyone saw me struggle, I would be a bad witness for Christ. That night Julie helped me realize that the Christian life isn't about being perfect; it's more about being transparent. It's about walking in God's strength and looking to him to help us through our shortcomings and failures, as we allow friends to walk beside us.

✿ ✿ ✿

Sharing our challenges allows others to pray with us and gives them the opportunity to see the power of God working in our lives. Trying to look perfect, on the other hand, only breeds frustration or envy in the people around us. We can't keep it up anyway, so why try? As Solomon said, "A man's pride brings him low, but a man of lowly spirit gains honor" (Proverbs 29:23).

What the World Needs to See

As Christians, the image we need people to see in us is that of someone whose life has been impacted by Christ's redemption and power. They may not see a perfect person, but they ought to see a forgiven person who trusts in God's strength and not her own.

It's easy to fall into the trap of thinking we need to maintain a perfect, holy image in order to be good witnesses for Christ. Don't misunderstand us; lifestyle is important. What we do and say is important. People do look at Christians to see what true Christianity is all about.

Hopefully what they see are people of love, joy, and righteous living. But they also need to see the reality that Christians do weep. They do mess up. And they, too, are in need of forgiveness.

Thankfully we have a God who knows our sinfulness and loves us just the same! We are the grateful receivers of God's abundant forgiveness, love, and power. That's the image the world needs from us.

In our relationships with our trusted friends, we need to be open, honest, and real. Relationships can go only so far with people who choose to hide who they really are. As we develop faithful, positive friendships, we need to share our hopes and dreams and abilities as well as our cares, concerns, and discouragements. No one wants to be best friends with a Polly Perfect type. What we really want is a friend we can relate to, a friend who understands.

Let's agree today to lay down our masks and allow our inner lights to shine with this positive message: "I'm loved and forgiven by a wonderful Savior and Friend! I don't need a mask, because he loves me just the way I am!"

POWER POINT

⚙ **Read:** 2 Corinthians 12:1–10. What could Paul boast about? (Glance back at chapter 11 for more insight.) How did Paul make himself vulnerable in this passage? What is the true picture Paul wanted people to see about his life, as expressed in verses 8–10?

♡ **Pray:** I praise you, Lord, for you are real! You have been open and honest with mankind from the beginning of time. You have revealed yourself to us in your Word and through the example of Christ's life on the earth. Thank you for allowing me to know you, and thank you that you can be trusted. Show me the masks I put on, and keep me from pretending to be something I'm not. Help me to be transparent to all who know me. Guide me in being open, honest, and real. Lead me to friends I can trust, and help me to be a trustworthy friend as well. I praise you for the way you work in my life; for when I am weak, you are strong. In Jesus' name I pray, amen.

♀ **Remember:** "Therefore I will boast all the more gladly about my weaknesses, so that Christ's power may rest on me" (2 Corinthians 12:9).

☺ **Do:** Look over the list of masks in this chapter. Do you see evidence of any of these masks in your life? Determine today to remove the mask and place it at Jesus' feet. Ask him to cover you with his image so that when people see you, they see God's redemptive power.

I can do everything Mask

Power Principle #7

THe Power OF forgiveness

Forgiveness is relinquishing my rights to hurt back.

—Archibald Hart

Bear with each other and forgive whatever grievances you may have against one another. Forgive as the Lord forgave you.

—Colossians 3:13

Mind Games
The Pitfalls of Assumptions and Judgments

Treat your friends as you do your picture,
and place them in their best light.

—Jennie Jerome Churchill

A sign posted on a bulletin board at a large factory reads: "To err is human; to forgive is not company policy."[1] Who would want to work for a company that never forgives mistakes? Yet many people hang a similar sign on the bulletin board of their hearts: "To err is human; to forgive is not my policy." Who would want to be friends with a person who never forgives faults?

We all make mistakes, and we all need forgiveness. Yet we all struggle at times to overlook each other's faults. Criticism and judgment—two characteristics that are deadly to any friendship—can flow all too easily from our hearts and minds.

If we're going to be positive friends, we need to learn to forgive faults and see the best in one another. First Corinthians 13, often called "the love chapter," tells us, "Love bears up under anything and everything that comes, is ever ready to believe the best of every person, its hopes are fadeless under all circumstances, and it endures everything [without weakening]" (1 Corinthians 13:7 AMP).

We're not suggesting that we stick our heads in the sand and ignore serious issues in our friends' lives that need to be addressed.

That's what chapter 14 was about—caring enough to confront the ones we love. But the flip side of caring enough to confront is loving our friends enough to overlook their faults and shortcomings and see the best in them. A positive friendship (and that includes a positive marriage) is based on the mutual understanding that we all are human. We all have frailties and shortcomings. We all make errors and mistakes—some more glaring than others. As positive friends, we need to forgive one another. We need to assume the best about each other, not the worst.

Dangerous Assumptions

It was December, and Debra was swamped. Not only did she have all the normal busyness that comes with being a wife and mother of two children during the holiday season, but she was in the middle of a huge project at work that needed to be completed before Christmas. On top of that, she had volunteered to direct her church's Christmas musical, and rehearsals were scheduled for several nights each week. Needless to say, Debra felt a little frazzled!

Meanwhile Debra's dearest friend, Suzette, was enjoying the holiday season at a much slower pace. Suzette worked part time from home as a makeup rep and volunteered at her kids' school twice a week. As Christmas approached, Suzette left a message on Debra's answering machine, asking when they could get together for their monthly lunch date. When she didn't hear from Debra for a couple of days, she e-mailed her with the same request.

Debra was so distracted by work, kids, home, and church that she forgot to return Suzette's phone call. And while she typically checked her e-mail regularly, she didn't have a chance to sit down at the computer for several days. Debra assumed Suzette would understand. But Suzette had some assumptions of her own. *Debra must be mad at me,*

Two persons cannot long be friends if they cannot forgive each other's little failings. —Jean de La Bruyere

Suzette thought, *and that's why she hasn't responded.* Suzette wracked her brain to figure out why Debra might be angry.

The only thing that came to mind was the fact that she had asked Debra several weeks earlier to host a makeup party for some of her office staff. Debra said she would do it, but not until January or February.

I bet Debra is mad because I'm trying to sell my makeup line to some of the women in her office, Suzette thought. *She thinks I'm using her. That has to be it!* Suzette began stewing. *If Debra doesn't support my line of work, how can she be a sincere friend? Maybe she's not the friend I thought she was!* And on and on went her thoughts—all based on one faulty assumption. Debra had no idea that a rift was developing; she was simply too busy to recognize there was a problem.

Before we judge Suzette too harshly, let's admit it: We all tend to make assumptions about people and situations. Our brains are constantly trying to solve for X, even when too many variables are missing to arrive at a valid answer. Often our assumptions are based on partial truths that we believe are the whole truth. An assumption about a thin girl leads to gossip about a possible eating disorder. A school board member prayerfully changes her stand on an issue and is assumed to be two-faced. A neighbor driving a luxury car is labeled extravagant, while another neighbor with an old, inexpensive vehicle is rumored to be hurting for cash.

Rather than asking questions and finding out the truth, we hang on to our assumptions and allow them to roll around in our minds, gaining weight and strength like a snowball rolling down a hill. Many times our assumptions prove to be false, but not before they roll off of our tongues in the form of gossip. Relationships are destroyed for reasons that turn out to be no reason at all.

The First Assumption

Our enemy, Satan, would love for us to feed on half-truths and assumptions. "Those delicious morsels are so tasty," he whispers to us, "and picking them is so easy!" Think back to the Garden of Eden and the destructive mind game Satan played with Adam and Eve. The first man and woman were enjoying perfect fellowship with God in the garden when Satan showed up in the form of a crafty serpent. He asked Eve a question to get the conversation going and the assumptions rolling: "Did God really say, 'You must not eat from any tree in the garden?'" (Genesis 3:1). Notice the toying with half-truths.

Eve responded with the facts: "We may eat fruit from the trees in the garden, but God did say, 'You must not eat fruit from the tree that is in the middle of the garden, and you must not touch it, or you will die'" (vv. 2–3). So far, so good.

Then the serpent declared a false speculation: "You will not surely die....For God knows that when you eat of it your eyes will be opened, and you will be like God, knowing good and evil" (vv. 4–5). Eve listened, and her mind began to assume that God was trying to keep something good from her. How often we are tempted to lose sight of God's unfailing love for us, and assume he does not care for us or have a great plan for our lives! Silly Eve. Silly us.

"When the woman saw that the fruit of the tree was good for food and pleasing to the eye, and also desirable for gaining wisdom, she took some and ate it. She also gave some to her husband, who was with her, and he ate it. Then the eyes of both of them were opened, and they realized they were naked; so they sewed fig leaves together and made coverings for themselves" (vv. 6–7). From Eve's perspective, the tree seemed good. From what she could tell, the fruit didn't appear to be deadly. And based on the serpent's words, she would gain wisdom if she ate it. Why would God hold this back from her? Surely she would not die! But death did enter the world when she sinned and ate from the forbidden tree. From that day until now, every person ever born has been under the curse of sin and death—all because of Eve's faulty assumption, which led her to doubt and disobey her Creator.

Hurt by Half-Truths

Half-truths and assumptions are like that—they often lead to death and destruction. Assumptions crashed the stock market in 1929. False speculations have started wars, demolished reputations, brought businesses to a halt. Assumptions based on false judgments caused an innocent man—the Son of God—to be nailed to a cross.

But assumptions don't just hurt other people. We hurt ourselves when we believe half-truths. We could spare ourselves so much emotional pain if we would search for the whole truth and allow our assumptions to fall away! A woman we pass in the hallway doesn't smile at us, so we assume she doesn't like us. Someone leans over and whispers to someone else, and we assume they are talking about us. A letter goes unanswered, and we assume the recipient has stopped caring. Nobody says anything about our new hair style, so we assume we look ugly. We get hurt—yet we've brought it on ourselves by believing our own assumptions.

Funny, isn't it, how many of our assumptions are all about us? We self-centeredly turn someone's unintentional comment or action into an intentional affront against us. If two friends are whispering, they must be saying something negative about us, right? It couldn't be that they're talking about their husbands, or the weather, or the surprise birthday party they want to throw for us because they love us. We need to recognize the difference between assumption and truth and be on constant guard against our tendency to assume things—especially negative things—based on partial truth or faulty information. A battle is going on in our heads, and we must decide what we choose to believe.

Second Corinthians 10:3–5 can be our battle cry:

> For though we walk in the flesh, we do not war according to the flesh, for the weapons of our warfare are not of the flesh, but divinely powerful for the destruction of fortresses. *We are* destroying speculations and every lofty thing raised up against the knowledge of God, and *we are* taking every thought captive to the obedience of Christ. (NASB)

Our responsibility is clear. If we want to be positive friends, we must hold on to truth, the whole truth, and nothing but the truth. As Jesus proclaimed, "You will know the truth, and the truth will set you free" (John 8:32). It's easy to get fuzzy in our thinking about what is true and what is merely assumed. Our job is to find out as many of the facts as we can and pray for God to give us discernment according to the truth. When we start camping on a particular thought, we need to ask, "Is this an assumption, or is it the complete truth?" We need to be continually asking God to make us aware of the faulty thinking that can so easily ensnare us.

Judgment Calls

One of the dangers of an assumption is that it can easily lead us to unfairly judge someone. It's so easy to slide from assumption or speculation to critical judgment. Somehow it makes us feel better when we can find something wrong with another person!

Why are we so quick to judge one another? For one thing, pride. Pride says, "I'm so glad I don't do *that.*" "I would never sin in *that* way." When we're filled with pride, we rarely see our own sin because we're so focused on finding everyone else's sin. Jesus warned us about the danger of judging one another in Matthew 7:1–5. Let's read this passage from the Amplified version to get a rich and full meaning:

> Do not judge *and* criticize *and* condemn others, so that you may not be judged *and* criticized *and* condemned yourselves.
>
> For just as you judge *and* criticize *and* condemn others, you will be judged *and* criticized *and* condemned, and in accordance with the measure you [use to] deal out to others, it will be dealt out again to you.
>
> Why do you stare from without at the very small particle that is in your brother's eye but do not become aware of *and* consider the beam of timber that is in your own eye?
>
> Or how can you say to your brother, Let me get the tiny particle out of your eye, when there is a beam of timber in your own eye?
>
> You hypocrite, first get the beam of timber out of your own eye, and then you will see clearly to take the tiny particle out of your brother's eye.

When we're prideful and judgmental, we get hung up on a person's sin, thinking how awful it is that she would sin in that way. We even hold on to the memory of the sin long after she has repented and moved on. Whenever we look at that person, we see the sin. The last thing we're thinking is how we can love, forgive, and help her.

If only we saw people with the grace-filled eyes of our loving heavenly Father! God knows that we are sinful. But through Christ he forgives us and helps us turn from our sin. When he looks at us, he doesn't see our sin; he sees who we are in Christ.

David gives us a beautiful picture of the way God views us in Psalm 103:1–14:

Praise the LORD, O my soul;

    all my inmost being, praise his holy name.

Praise the LORD, O my soul,

    and forget not all his benefits—

who forgives all your sins

    and heals all your diseases,

who redeems your life from the pit

    and crowns you with love and compassion,

who satisfies your desires with good things

    so that your youth is renewed like the eagle's.

The LORD works righteousness

    and justice for all the oppressed.

He made known his ways to Moses,

    his deeds to the people of Israel:

The LORD is compassionate and gracious,

    slow to anger, abounding in love.

He will not always accuse,

    nor will he harbor his anger forever;

he does not treat us as our sins deserve

    or repay us according to our iniquities.

For as high as the heavens are above the earth,

    so great is his love for those who fear him;

as far as the east is from the west,

    so far has he removed our transgressions from us.

As a father has compassion on his children,

    so the LORD has compassion on those who fear him;

for he knows how we are formed,

    he remembers that we are dust.

If God looks upon us and treats us in such a loving way, how can we do any less for our fellow human beings—and especially our friends? God knows we are dust, yet he lovingly forgives us and removes our transgressions from us. Sadly, we are not always so generous. Many Christians even claim to act in the name of God when they accuse and condemn others. To hold one another accountable and help each other turn from sin is one thing, but to judge one another in self-righteous pride is another thing altogether. Pride, criticism, and judgment should have no place in our lives if we want to be positive friends and true reflections of God's love.

Neither should jealousy. We already talked about the destructive force of jealousy in chapter 10; we'll simply note here that, in addition to pride, jealousy is a major root that leads to judging and criticizing others. Recognizing our own jealousies is not always easy. We need to do a continuous systems check to make sure the "ugly green monster" has not snuck into our hearts and minds and set up camp.

Is there someone you have been critical of in the past few months? Do you find yourself thinking that a friend's success is unfair? Do you wish you had her hair, facial features, body (and the list could go on)? Are you envious of her gifts, talents, abilities, or awards?

If you recognize jealousy in your heart, take it before the Lord right now. Confess it to God. Thank him for the way he made you and the gifts he has given you. Then go the next step and thank the Lord for blessing your friend. Yes, you read that right! As we release our feelings of jealousy to God, we begin to see that our loving heavenly Father has a plan for our lives as well as for our friends' lives. We don't need to waste time worrying about the path God has set for someone else. Instead, we must keep our eyes on Jesus and on the unique and wonderful path he has set for us.

He who cannot forgive others destroys the bridge over which he himself must pass. —George Herbert

Appreciating Differences

Sometimes we judge one another not because we're prideful or jealous, but simply because we're different. Remember the personality types we talked about in chapter 2? People with different personality types handle situations and respond to other people differently. It's easy to misunderstand and judge someone who doesn't do things the same way we do.

Take Maxine Melancholy, the organizer of the ladies luncheon at church. She was chosen to head the committee because she is very organized, punctual, and loves attending to details. Two months before the luncheon, she began scheduling weekly planning meetings for Tuesday mornings at 10:00 A.M. sharp. She was always in the church meeting room at least fifteen minutes ahead of time. But one of the committee members, Sally Sanguine, flew in every week at about 10:15, usually with a colorful story explaining why she was late. After the fourth week of listening to Sally's excuses, Maxine was ready to boil over.

Why can't Sally be on time? she thought. *These meetings are a serious matter. They should be a top priority to everyone on the committee. Obviously, Sally has her priorities out of line. She needs to get her life in order!*

To make matters worse, as Maxine conducted the meetings, Sally frequently tried to interject creative and fun new ideas. Finally Maxine blurted out, "Sally, we have always done the luncheon this way. This is how it works best. We are not going to change something that works just fine."

Sally's usual smile vanished. *Who appointed Maxine queen of the luncheon?* she thought. *Can't she think outside the box—even just a little? If she prayed about it, I know she'd recognize that God does things creatively.*

Can you see what was happening? Sally was judging Maxine while Maxine was judging Sally. Neither one was wrong about how to plan the luncheon; they were simply acting according to the way they were created. Instead of judging one another, however, the two women could have built on each other's strengths and employed their God-given talents and gifts in a complementary way. But sadly, they were so caught up in judging that they missed the potential blessing.

Vengeance Is the Lord's

When people hurt or offend us in some way, our natural tendency is to try to get back at them. We think it's our job to repay them for the wrong that they have done. Hey, we're already playing judge; shouldn't we administer the punishment as well? The deep-down desire for revenge is so common to the human experience that it has been the subject of countless novels through the centuries, not to mention many modern movies. We can all relate.

Revenge comes in many shapes and sizes. Joan doesn't invite Carla to Ladies Night Out, because Carla's daughter left Joan's daughter out of the group at school. Steve doesn't shop at Tom's hardware store, because Tom doesn't use Steve's security company. Nancy always seems to be nice to everyone but Rhonda, so Rhonda assigns Nancy to the worst time slot at work.

What does the Bible have to say about revenge and getting back at others? Romans 12:17–20 speaks clearly to the issue:

Do not repay anyone evil for evil. Be careful to do what is right in the eyes of everybody. If it is possible, as far as it depends on you, live at peace with everyone. Do not take revenge, my friends, but leave room for God's wrath, for it is written: "It is mine to avenge; I will repay," says the Lord. On the contrary:

"If your enemy is hungry, feed him;
　　if he is thirsty, give him something to drink.
In doing this, you will heap burning coals on his head."

257

Paul closes Romans 12 with these final words in verse 21: "Do not be overcome by evil, but overcome evil with good." Isn't that what our motto ought to be for dealing with both our friends and our enemies and everyone in between? Do not be overcome with evil—judging, making assumptions, harboring jealousy, seeking revenge—but overcome evil with good. Bless all of the people in your life. Pray for them. Be kind to them. Simply put, see them as God sees them and love them as God loves them. If you do that, you'll be a positive friend indeed.

POWER POINT

⚙ **Read:** Matthew 9:1–13, 32–34. How many false assumptions were made about Jesus in these passages? Were any of the assumptions based on truth? What do you think was at the root of these misjudgments?

🕊 **Pray:** Faithful and true heavenly Father, thank you for your forgiveness and love. Help me extend that same forgiveness and love to other people, especially my friends. Guard my mind from making false assumptions. Keep me from judging others unfairly. Give me wisdom to see things clearly in all my friendships. Help me make a difference in the lives of others by being a faithful and forgiving friend. In Jesus' name I pray, amen.

💡 **Remember:** "Do not judge, or you too will be judged" (Matthew 7:1).

☺ **Do:** Take time to examine your heart and mind. Have you made an assumption about someone that's not based on the whole truth? Have you judged a friend or acquaintance out of pride or jealousy—or simply because that person is different from you? Release that judgment to God and allow his love and grace to flow through you. On the flip side, has anyone made a false assumption or accusation against you? Ask God to help you forgive that person today.

17

Grace Received, Grace Given
The Forgiveness Factor

When we forgive someone we don't change him or her, but ourselves.
We liberate ourselves from all obligations to continuing bitterness. This
doesn't reverse the past. But it changes the present and the future.

—Forrest Church

Tears streamed down Nick's freckled, eight-year-old cheeks. Through the windows of his mom's Explorer, he watched as all the boys from his class piled into the minivan parked next to him. They were all going to John's birthday party. Everyone but him.

Nick's mother looked on in disbelief from the driver's seat. Surely there must have been a mistake. The invitation must have been lost in the mail.

"Stay in the car," she told Nick, her heart heavy. "I'm going to dash in to speak with your teacher." She hoped Mrs. Kirkland could shed some light on the situation.

Mrs. Kirkland listened as Nick's mom explained what had just happened in the school parking lot.

"Yes, there must have been a mistake," the kindhearted teacher confirmed. "John even prayed out loud in class today that all of the boys would have a good time at his party."

"And besides, Nick is probably the most liked child in the class," she added. "He's even kind to the girls—which is amazing because most boys at this age think that girls are 'yucky.'"

259

She quickly picked up the phone in her classroom to call John's parents. "I'm sure Nick is supposed to be there," she said. But when John's dad answered and was presented with the dilemma, he gave a reply that nobody expected.

"Our home is very small," he said matter-of-factly. "My wife invited only seven of the nine boys in the class."

That was it. No "I'm sorry." No "Oh, please bring him on over. We never meant to hurt the boys who were left out." Nothing. Mrs. Kirkland hung up the phone and in disbelief relayed the message to Nick's mom.

Only a mother can appreciate how her heart ached for her son as she made her way back to the car. "Help me, Lord," she prayed, "to tell him the truth in a way that will help him understand something I can't comprehend myself." She opened the car door, slid behind the wheel, and turned to face his hope-filled eyes.

"Nick," she began, her eyes stinging as she fought back her own tears, "John's house is very small, so he couldn't invite everyone. I'm sure he likes you very much…"

She couldn't continue. She watched his hope turn to disappointment and then give way to deep sobs of rejection. Quickly she moved to him and tenderly drew him to herself. A flood of anger engulfed her. *How could anyone, especially another mother, be so cruel?*

"I'm never going to invite John to one of my birthday parties!" Nick suddenly lashed out through his sobs.

His mom was tempted to agree. But she knew she had to rein in her own anger in order to help her son. "What do you think Jesus would do?" she asked quietly. "Don't you think he would want you to forgive John?"

Nick didn't answer.

That day came and went. Not another word was said about the incident. The next morning, with lunch in hand and backpack in tow,

Nick set off for school. All day long his mother couldn't get the picture of her sobbing son out of her mind. As each hour passed, she grew angrier. She didn't want Nick to get into an altercation with John, but she found herself hoping that he would at least ignore his classmate and give him the silent treatment.

Imagine her surprise when she picked him up from school at three, and Nick bounced into the car, his face beaming.

"Mom, guess what?" his words tumbled out. "I asked John if his party was fun. He said it was, and then he played with me at recess! I asked him if he wanted to come to my birthday party when I have it, and he said he did."

Nick's attitude toward his friend can only be explained with one word: forgiveness. What is it about children that causes them to love so freely and forgive so unconditionally? Maybe it has something to do with the fact that when they are very young, they have no hidden agendas; they take everything at face value. They haven't yet built up a history of the pain inflicted by broken promises, underhanded tactics, and impure motives. That's why we call them "innocent." Their innocence permits them to see a wrongdoing in a parent or friend and decide the offender simply made a mistake.

It takes only a few years, however, for these trusting, loving, and forgiving children to become wary. They slowly wise up (if you want to call it that) and realize that the world is not always nice. They begin to understand that the people around them are sometimes thoughtlessly or purposely mean.

This new awareness has some benefits. Now they can begin to analyze people and situations based on past experiences. Hopefully they can use this growing ability to discern in a way that will help them make wise choices in life. The danger is that this new realization about the ways of the world will cause them to judge *people* rather than *behavior*. When we judge people instead of judging their behavior, we leave little room for forgiveness.

Jesus was able to see past sinful behavior to the individual who was wonderfully created by God. He hated the sin, but he loved the sinner. He took a firm, unwavering stand against thoughts and actions that were unholy, while still offering unmerited forgiveness to anyone who repented. We can't grant eternal forgiveness to others; that kind of forgiveness produces eternal redemption, and it can only be granted by God. However, we can grant the kind of forgiveness that allows our friendships to be restored—if we will restrict our judgment to the offense and not the person.

There's another reason many of us find it difficult to forgive, especially when the offender is a friend or family member. We tend to see an offense as a personal attack on our lives designed to thwart our success and cause us pain. Our perspective is limited and small. We fail to look at our life circumstances from God's point of view. Instead of living out the truth that "in all things God works for the good of those who love him, who have been called according to his purpose" (Romans 8:28), we tend to be shortsighted. We question God, wondering why he would allow such an unfair event or circumstance to happen to us.

It's not wrong to ask God why. But when we allow questioning to become a permanent state of mind, then we have crossed the line. Now we are doubting God's authority over our lives. We are doubting his supreme love and care for us. We are saying, "God, I know what's best for my life, and this is not it!"

Joseph: A Giant of Forgiveness

One of the most poignant and illustrative examples of trusting God in the face of adversity—to the point that forgiving those who have wronged us is simply a byproduct of our faith—is found in the first book of the Bible. The historical account of Joseph in the Book of Genesis is filled with intrigue, jealousy, pride, betrayal, suffering, and grief. It's also filled with trust, loyalty, humility, devotion, forgiveness, and restoration.

Let's take a quick peek into the life of someone whose heart was so wholly devoted to God that even unjust suffering was met with complete trust that God knew best. This knowledge kept Joseph from wallowing in bitterness and freed him to forgive those who had set out to destroy his life.

Joseph was the eleventh of twelve sons born to Jacob, who was himself the grandson of the great patriarch, Abraham. Jacob loved Joseph, the Scripture tells us, more than he did the rest of his children. He demonstrated his favor in such a way that Joseph's brothers, as you might expect, became extremely jealous. (There is a great lesson about showing favoritism here. Jacob's favoritism didn't lend itself to brotherly bonding, to say the least.)

In Genesis 37:3–4 we read, "Now Israel [also known as Jacob] loved Joseph more than any of his other sons, because he had been born to him in his old age; and he made a richly ornamented robe for him. When his brothers saw that their father loved him more than any of them, they hated him and could not speak a kind word to him."

Joseph didn't help the situation any when he shared one of his dreams with his brothers. The Scripture continues: "Joseph had a dream, and when he told it to his brothers, they hated him all the more. He said to them, 'Listen to this dream I had: We were binding sheaves of grain out in the field when suddenly my sheaf rose and stood upright, while your sheaves gathered around mine and bowed down to it" (vv. 5–7).

By this point the brothers had reached the height of sibling rivalry.

They'd had their fill of their father's favoritism and what was, from their perspective, their cocky little brother's arrogance and pride. Their jealousy gave way to resentment, which gave way to hatred, which ultimately led to rejection and betrayal. Nine of the brothers conspired to kill Joseph; but Reuben, the oldest, intervened and suggested they throw their youngest sibling into a pit instead. How kind of him!

As if being thrown in a pit weren't bad enough, Joseph's life was about to take a terrible turn for the worse—all at the hands of his own flesh and blood. The brothers decided to sell Joseph to a caravan of traveling merchants that happened to pass by. The merchants in turn sold him to a high-ranking official in Egypt named Potiphar.

Joseph didn't wallow in his misery or allow bitterness to paralyze him. Trusting God in the midst of his circumstances, he began working for his new master as unto the Lord. Before long, Potiphar became so impressed with Joseph's work that he put him in charge of running his entire household.

But once again, Joseph was "sold out" by those he trusted. Potiphar's wife decided she needed a boyfriend—despite her wedding ring—and began making advances toward Joseph. God's man stood firm and refused her. But where do you think that got him? Potiphar believed his wife's story that Joseph was the aggressor, and he threw his favored servant back into a pit: the pit of prison.

At that point Joseph—bewildered, hurt, and surely discouraged—did the unnatural thing once again. He chose to live his life, despite being misunderstood, as unto the Lord. His attitude in the face of adversity garnered him the approval of the prison warden, who put Joseph in charge of all the other prisoners. Ultimately, through a series of events that could only have been orchestrated by God, Joseph was released from prison and rose to become the ruler of all of Egypt, second in command only to Pharaoh himself!

When a famine hit Joseph's homeland, his family—Jacob and his brothers who'd sold him into slavery—were confronted with possible starvation. His brothers were forced to travel to Egypt to beg for food from the Egyptian ruler. Not recognizing that Joseph was their long-lost brother, they bowed before him, just as Joseph's childhood dream had foretold, and pleaded for assistance.

The ultimate test of forgiveness had arrived. Although Joseph had, over the years, accepted God's plan for his life, he was now face to face with those who had inflicted so much pain upon him. Their fate was now in his hands, and he had options.

Option number one: He could repay evil with evil. Just the thought of retribution must have brought delight to Joseph's mind. Over the years he must have imagined what it would be like to confront the traitors. But clearly Joseph did not allow these thoughts to consume his mind and heart; if he had, he would have been rendered useless in the hands of God. His sights were placed on trusting God and living to please him.

Option number two: He could forgive those who had greatly wronged him, recognizing that his fate rested ultimately in the loving hands of the God he served. Joseph was wise. He was able to look back over his life and see that in the midst of a variety of unjust circumstances marked by rejection, demotion, pain, and humiliation, God had been actively working to elevate Joseph to the place where he could best serve him.

True to character, Joseph picked what was behind door number two and freely forgave his brothers. Not only did he forgive them, he also chose to bless them beyond measure. Financially, he gave them everything they needed and more. But he also did something far more significant than meeting their physical needs: He restored their fellowship. He gave them a home and a place of honor in Egypt, no strings

And when you stand praying, if you hold anything against anyone, forgive him, so that your Father in heaven may forgive you your sins. —Mark 11:25

attached, as well as an unconditional home in his heart.

What about you? Where are you in your pilgrimage of forgiveness? Do you tend to see the wrong inflicted on you by others from the perspective of "poor pitiful me"? Or are you able to wade through the hurt feelings and anger and desire for revenge to get to the place of resting in God's will for your life? As Joseph learned, only when we are able to give our broken, angry, and vengeful hearts to God—the one who is able to make all things right in his timing—are we then free to forgive!

The Cost of Unforgiveness

We don't know about you, but at times we have almost enjoyed hanging on to an unforgiving spirit. If someone wrongs one of our children or spouse, a mentality rises up within us that says, "I'm going to show that person that he (or she) can't mess with my family!" For a moment, we feel a sense of satisfaction—but it's always short-lived. We've learned that over time an unforgiving spirit will rob us of joy and peace. It will begin to consume us with thoughts of revenge. If left unchecked, it will bring us to the point of no longer enjoying the sweet, simple things in life that used to bring us pleasure. An unforgiving spirit is like an emotional ball and chain that we lug around day in and day out. Its cumbersome weight can make every activity a drudgery.

Terry Ann reflects: Recently my mother-in-law, Dixie, shared with me her own journey toward forgiveness. It started almost twenty years ago when she received a phone call late one night. It was every mother's nightmare: Her oldest son, Bob, my husband's big brother, had been killed. Bob had been at a party, and an uninvited guest had shown up and shot him for no apparent reason.

Months passed before the police were able to apprehend the fugitive; and with each passing day, Dixie's denial turned to despair and ultimately to feelings of rage and revenge. She became so obsessed with hatred for the killer that every area in her life was affected. No matter how hard she struggled to let go, she just couldn't free herself from the prison of unforgiveness.

A breakthrough came in the form of a wise and caring friend, who asked Dixie this question: "If God worked a miracle and wanted to give you the ability to forgive your son's murderer, would you receive the gift of forgiveness?" Dixie couldn't answer. She realized that up to that point, not only could she not forgive the man, but she didn't want to forgive him if she could!

She continued to mull over her friend's question, however. And after much prayer and deep introspection, she reached the point where she felt ready to pray, "Lord, if you are able to work the huge miracle of allowing me to forgive, I will by faith accept it."

Like Joseph, Dixie had options. She had choices about what to do with her feelings of hatred and revenge. Her heart was far from forgiveness, but she made the mental decision to forgive anyway. She was tired of the struggle. She knew her anger had taken a huge toll, robbing her of years of joyful living. She turned to God and accepted his gift.

The feelings of forgiveness didn't settle in overnight but over time. God was faithful, and the joy of the Lord now resides in a heart that once was home to all the destructive emotions of unforgiveness.

❖ ❖ ❖

You probably haven't had to struggle with forgiving the kind of offense that Dixie had to forgive. But all of us have been hurt at one time or another by family, friend, or foe. What happens with that hurt boils down to one word: choice. We all have a choice. Are we willing to allow God to give us the grace to forgive? What have we got to lose?

When we're not willing to let go of our bitterness, we injure no one but ourselves. The ones who hurt us probably haven't lost one night of sleep over the offense; and here we are, being eaten away on the inside, to the point of being miserable day and night!

But there is even a greater reason to forgive besides restoring our emotional well-being God commands it! Throughout Scripture we are called to forgive every individual who wrongs us. Let's take a look at just a few of God's commands concerning forgiveness:

> Get rid of all bitterness, rage and anger, brawling and slander, along with every form of malice. Be kind and compassionate to one another, forgiving each other, just as in Christ God forgave you. (Ephesians 4:31–32)

> Bear with each other and forgive whatever grievances you may have against one another. Forgive as the Lord forgave you. (Colossians 3:13)

> Do not judge, and you will not be judged. Do not condemn, and you will not be condemned. Forgive, and you will be forgiven. (Luke 6:37)

God's command to forgive is clear, and so is his reason: We're to forgive because he, in his mercy and grace, has forgiven us. But notice the verse we just quoted from Luke 6. Receiving that forgiveness is contingent upon us forgiving others! Wow! Jesus couldn't have been any plainer when he said, "For if you forgive men when they sin against you, your heavenly Father will also forgive you. But if you do not forgive men their sins, your Father will not forgive your sins" (Matthew 6:14–15). Never underestimate the power of forgiveness!

Oh yes, we have options. We can be obedient to God, forgive, be forgiven, and live within God's plan for our lives; or we can be disobedient to God, choose not to forgive or be forgiven, and live outside of God's perfect plan.

Forgiveness isn't easy. It's a struggle for all of us. Sometimes we try to make it easier on ourselves by adding stipulations: "Well, I guess I'll forgive her if she comes to me with tears in her eyes and is really repentant. After all, God forgave me of my sins after I came to him in repentance." For many of us, this kind of thinking makes perfect sense. Wasn't our own forgiveness contingent on our repentance?

Well, let's take a look at what God's Word has to say. In Romans 5:6–8 we read, "You see, at just the right time, when we were still powerless, Christ died for the ungodly. Very rarely will anyone die for a righteous man, though for a good man someone might possibly dare to die. But God demonstrates his own love for us in this: While we were still sinners, Christ died for us." God made provision for our forgiveness before we ever came to him in repentance!

It's clear. We are to forgive our family members, friends, and even our enemies for two reasons: because God commands it, and because we are emotionally healthier when we let go of bitterness and revenge. Releasing the negative feelings that keep us in bondage becomes easier as we think about the unmerited forgiveness that God has granted to us. Consider the sinful thoughts, desires, and attitudes that we harbor in our hearts every single day. God forgives us for all of these—the very sins that nailed his perfect Son to the cross! How can we not forgive the lady down the street for not inviting us to her luncheon or our employer for not giving us the promotion we think we deserved?

Project Elephant

We all have times when we need to be forgiven—by God most of all, but also by others.

❀

Terry Ann reflects: My most vivid memory of my own need for forgiveness goes back to my days as an overly talkative, bright-eyed, chubby-cheeked, blonde-haired six-year-old in Mrs. Maxie's first grade class. That's where I learned how to read with those "Dick and Jane" readers. (Remember "See Spot run. Run, Spot, run"?) It's also where I learned simple addition and subtraction. And it's where I learned how to get along better with others.

I also learned something else in first grade that was more important than all of those things put together.

One particular day Mrs. Maxie gave us what sounded like a fun assignment. We were asked to draw an elephant with a caravan on top (you know, a *caravan*—that thing that people sit in when they ride on top of the elephant). Well, I was quickly frustrated beyond belief, because in my whole six years of living I'd never developed an expertise in drawing elephants. I was confident that I could draw the caravan-thingy on top with a little man in it, but the elephant was simply beyond my reach.

I glanced over at the paper of my little schoolroom neighbor, Robin. Her elephant was incredible! I couldn't believe it. She was truly an *artiste magnifico.* So I asked her to draw my elephant. No big deal—after all, I would draw the rest myself. She agreed. She drew. I said, "Thank you." Project Elephant complete.

Then came the moment of truth. Some very distinguished and discriminating judges entered our classroom to choose the best elephants to proudly hang on display—in some extremely prestigious art museum, I think. Well, guess what? My elephant was chosen as one of the very best, and Robin's was passed by. Off went my masterpiece into the art fair corridors, a shoe-in to lead me to the heights of the art community. When the months passed and I left the first grade, it was with the reputation of *artiste extraordinaire.*

That summer my sisters and I spent most of the hottest days riding to and from the community swimming pool in our wood-paneled station wagon. While sitting in the back seat on one of our swimming outings, I surprised everyone by suddenly bursting into tears.

"It wasn't my elephant!" I cried.

"What elephant?" Mother said, looking at me from the rear view mirror.

"The one that was chosen for the art fair. I didn't draw it. Robin did."

I'll never forget the look on my mother's face. It was one of horror, dismay, and disappointment, all rolled into one. And then she spoke the words that have been etched in my psyche for over thirty-five years: "You'll have to go to Mrs. Maxie when school starts back up and confess it. Then you must ask her to forgive you for cheating and lying."

Needless to say, I lived in fear of having to start the second grade. But the day came. We were all back at school. We were in our lunch period, and the lights in the cafeteria had been turned off. (The principal did this whenever we got too loud.) That's when I saw her: Mrs. Maxie, sitting with her new group of ever-so-immature first graders.

The dreaded moment was upon me. I made my move (in the dark, mind you) and walked stealthily over to my old teacher. I tapped her on the shoulder and then sobbed out the words "It wasn't my elephant!"

Despite my hysterics, sweet Mrs. Maxie figured out the reason for my guilt and remorse. I vividly remember her loving embrace as she graciously extended the gift of forgiveness. Finally my six-year-old, guilt-ravaged heart was free.

❀ ❀ ❀

What about you? Is there someone you need to go to in order to ask forgiveness? Or are you the one who needs to do the forgiving?

As Christians and as positive friends, we need to be cultivating truly forgiving hearts. How do we do that? Ultimately the answer is by the power of God's Holy Spirit working in us as we recognize how much we've been forgiven by God. To help us along, however, we like Robert Muller's idea of setting up a schedule of forgiveness. It might look something like this:

Sunday: Forgive yourself.

Monday: Forgive your family.

Tuesday: Forgive your friends and associates.

Wednesday: Forgive across economic lines within your nation.

Thursday: Forgive across cultural lines within your own own nation.

Friday: Forgive across political lines within your own nation.

Saturday: Forgive other nations.[1]

Because it's not easy, forgiveness sometimes takes discipline—and courage. Sometimes we want to hold on to unforgiveness like a security blanket. We feel that if we forgive, we'll only get hurt again. That's why Muller says, "Only the brave know how to forgive. A coward never forgives. It's not in his nature."[2]

As positive friends, we need to go to God and ask him for the courage and strength to forgive. There is no sweeter gift that we can give a friend or receive from a friend than the gift of forgiveness. We need to forgive for our friends' sakes, for our own sakes, and for Christ's sake. Forgiveness builds bridges and works miracles in the lives of both the forgiver and the forgiven. And a heart full of forgiveness brings glory to God.

POWER POINT

⚙ **Read:** Matthew 18:21–35. How often should we forgive someone who has sinned against us? What was so disgusting about the actions of the forgiven servant? Have you ever been like him? What reason does this passage give us for forgiving others?

Pray: Glorious, loving, and forgiving heavenly Father, I praise you for your abundant love and powerful forgiveness. How marvelous and freeing it is to know that I am forgiven in your sight! Thank you for the price you paid for my forgiveness: the life of your only Son. I am grateful and humbled. You gave such a great sacrifice for me, may I never hold something against another person! Free me from the prison of unforgiveness, and remind me if there is anyone I need to go to in order to ask for forgiveness. Thank you for giving me the power and strength to forgive—especially when it seems impossible. In Jesus' name and for his sake I pray, amen.

Remember: "Be kind and compassionate to one another, forgiving each other, just as in Christ God forgave you" (Ephesians 4:32).

Do: Examine your heart. Do you bear unforgiveness toward a particular friend? Lay down that stronghold right now and forgive her, whether she has asked for forgiveness or not. Ask God to help you to forgive, and ask him to heal any wounds that remain as a result of the offense.

Is there a friend you need to go to in order to ask forgiveness? Even if the offense occurred years ago, don't put it off. Do it today.

Conclusion

In Search of the Perfect Friend
Who Fits the Bill?

The love of God toward you is like the Amazon River flowing down to water a single daisy.

—F. B. Meyer

An old Turkish proverb says, "He who seeks a perfect friend remains without one." It's funny how most of us deep down inside hope to find a friend that fits us perfectly and doesn't seem to have any faults. Let's admit it, we did that in looking for a husband, but we soon learned that even a seemingly perfect mate can have at least a few glaring flaws. You would think that if we wrote the book on positive friendship, that our friendship would border on perfection. We may as well set the story straight, there have been times when we were not the picture-perfect friends to each other.

❀

Terry Ann reflects: It began many years ago when Karol called and told me with great excitement that she had just received a contract from a big-name publisher to write her very first book. I was truly in awe that my dear friend was going to be in print. I was happy for her!

To show my interest, I began quizzing Karol about the details. Did the publisher consider the book a high priority, or was it simply a "filler" that would not be given much promotion? Would the company be putting a substantial amount of money into the paper stock? Did the advance she would be receiving give an indication of how much faith the publisher was putting in her manuscript?

Can you believe I asked her all that? I was no expert, believe me. But it just so happened that not long before Karol's call, an acquaintance had been telling me about the hierarchy that publishers set up for their books, and the issue was fresh on my mind.

Karol was quite unaware of the way that publishers rank books, however, so my questions were rather alarming to her. Through my insensitive interrogation (which, even as I write this, I feel embarrassed about), I determined that Karol's book was most likely a C book in the ABC ranking. The incredible thing is, I told her this. What was I thinking? I was clueless that I might be treading on sensitive ground for a new author. I figured that Karol and I were good friends, so she would know that I wanted the details for the sole purpose of getting a better understanding of the world of publishing.

It may be hard for you to believe, but I really was happy for Karol, and I had no idea that my questions were hurting her feelings. I mean, she never let on. She acted a bit stunned, and at times the long lapse between my brilliant questions and her two and three word answers did seem a little odd. It was uncharacteristic of Karol to be at a loss for words. But then, what did I know? Maybe she had something important on her mind (like how to tell off a friend without sinning!). She never acted offended—although she did cut the phone conversation a little short, as I recall.

Several months later Karol called to ask if I could help her out. She had accepted an invitation to speak to a church group on the topic "Friendship in the Fast Lane" and later found out that her husband had planned a trip for the two of them for that very week. Could I possibly fill in for her?

I checked my calendar and saw that the date was clear. I told Karol that I would be glad to help, then asked a favor of my own. Could she send me the notes she'd already put together so I wouldn't have to start from scratch? I promised to simply read them to help me get the creative juices flowing for my own speech.

Without reservation Karol sent me the notes, and I eagerly read away. The manuscript was filled with page after page of excellent thoughts on the importance of being a good and positive friend. I was thoroughly enjoying myself, until I got to a passage that made me stop dead in my literary tracks. There in black and white was this sentence: "I'll never forget how I had to forgive the insensitivity and cruel remarks of a dear friend." In the next sentence, I saw my own name: "When I told Terry Ann about my exciting new book deal, instead of rejoicing with me and encouraging me, she continued to question the significance of my writing. She made sure that I knew that my book was of little worth."

I had to literally catch my breath. Immediately I began trying to reconstruct the conversation from months ago. *Is that how I came across to Karol?* I asked myself. *How could she have ever gleaned that from our conversation? Wow, was I really that insensitive?*

Clearly I hadn't followed Power Principle #2. I was a failure when it came to encouraging my friend and cheering her on from the sidelines. But I wasn't the only imperfect friend in the matter. Karol had definitely violated Power Principle #6. She hadn't been honest with me. She didn't lovingly confront me. And just in case you're keeping score, she also violated Power Principle #7 regarding forgiveness. Specifically, she made false assumptions regarding my intentions and judged me based on those assumptions.

One up for me, right? Not! Neither of us is a perfect person. That means, as hard as we might try, we're not perfect friends. But at least we have our imperfection in common! And just to let you know, Karol forgave my insensitivity long ago, and I forgave her too. Today our relationship is probably stronger because of the struggle we had to go through to work maturely through this situation.

❖   ❖   ❖

Positive or Perfect?

A positive friend is not a perfect friend. None of us is perfect. But we can still have positive friendships. A positive friendship is one in which two people help each other be all that God created them to be. They bless each other through their words and actions and by simply being there for one another. Do they fall short? You bet! Do they struggle at times? Without at doubt! The important thing is that they love each other and continue to build their relationship using the principles we have shared in this book.

For example, they base their friendship on common bonds. They try to be encouragers. They make every effort to be givers, not takers—although they know how to receive graciously. They are loyal in all of their words and actions. They delight in the fellowship that comes from shared faith. They seek to be open and honest and real and to forgive continually.

Wouldn't it be great if we could all be positive friends all the time? But recognizing that we may fail, isn't it comforting to know that God can pick us up, dust us off, and keep us growing? He doesn't promise us that we will be perfect (at least, not this side of heaven), but he does assure us that "[H]is divine power has given us everything we need for life and godliness" (2 Peter 1:3). In reality, there is only one perfect friend. God himself is the one and only true and positive friend we will ever have.

His Divine Nature

Notice how God himself embodies the principles we have talked about in this book.

The Power of Forgiveness

How glorious it is to know that God our heavenly Father forgives us of our sins! We all need to be forgiven; we all do wrong things. But God offers us his powerful love and healing grace through the gift of forgiveness. Ephesians 1:7–8 speaks about this wonderful gift: "In him we have redemption through his blood, the forgiveness of sins, in accordance with the riches of God's grace that he lavished on us with all wisdom and understanding." Through the blood of Christ, God lovingly labels us *forgiven*.

The Power of Honesty

Deuteronomy 32:4 gives us a bold description of God: "He is the Rock, his work is perfect: for all his ways are judgment: a God of truth and without iniquity, just and right is he" (KJV). In the New Testament Jesus declared, "I am the way and the truth and the life" (John 14:6). God is a God of truth. Honesty is his nature. He cannot lie. How wonderful it is to know that we can trust him and his Word!

The Power of Spiritual Bonds

Obviously God is the origin of all spiritual bonds. Because we have his Holy Spirit working in our lives, we can connect with him on a deep level, a heart level, and not simply a surface level. Have you ever thought about the incredible gift God has given us in his Spirit? We are not alone to live out our lives in our own strength or wisdom, because God has given us his Spirit to live within us. Read with joy 1 Corinthians 2:10–13:

> The Spirit searches all things, even the deep things of God. For who among men knows the thoughts of a man except the man's spirit within him? In the same way no one knows the thoughts of God except the Spirit of God. We have not received the spirit of the world but the Spirit who is from God, that we may understand what God has freely given us. This is what we speak, not in words taught us by human wisdom but in words taught by the Spirit, expressing spiritual truths in spiritual words.

It's a marvelous spiritual truth: We have a spiritual connection with God when we put our faith in Christ and allow his Spirit to fill our lives.

The Power of Loyalty

God has many outstanding qualities, but perhaps one of the most reassuring to us is that he is faithful. David declared, "Your love, O LORD, reaches to the heavens, your faithfulness to the skies" (Psalm 36:5). Deuteronomy 7:9 says, "Know therefore that the LORD your God is God; he is the faithful God, keeping his covenant of love to a thousand generations of those who love him and keep his commands." He will never leave us nor abandon us. He can be trusted. Oh, the comfort of knowing that his unfailing love abides with us forever! No other friend is as loyal, faithful, and true.

The Power of Giving

Some people think of God as a taker, foolishly assuming that if they give their lives to God, he will take away their money, their pleasure, and their fun in life. But God is a giver. He gave his only Son so that "whoever believes in him shall not perish but have eternal life" (John 3:16). He gives us forgiveness. He gives us eternal hope and a peace that passes all understanding. He gives us purpose and significance. He gives us unfailing love. He is the giver of all good gifts and eternal blessings!

The Power of Encouragement

The word *encourage* means to give strength. God gives his followers strength for the journey. He is an encourager, not a discourager. Listen to the encouraging words he spoke to Joshua when Joshua became the leader of the Israelite tribes: "Be strong and courageous, because you will lead these people to inherit the land I swore to their forefathers to give them....Have I not commanded you? Be strong and courageous. Do not be terrified; do not be discouraged, for the LORD your God will be with you wherever you go" (Joshua 1:6, 9).

Now *that's* a powerful dose of encouragement coming from the one who can truly give strength. And he is saying the same words to us today: "Be strong! Be courageous! I am with you!" May we receive and be grateful for the courage he gives us through his love, his Word, and the friends he sends our way!

The Power of Sisterhood

You're probably wondering how we're going to connect God with the principle of the power of sisterhood. But really, it's quite easy. Women can understand each other in a way that men can't begin to fathom, right? (That's OK, we don't claim to understand them either!) Well, God is our designer and creator. No one knows our wants, needs, hopes, and dreams better than he does. He can completely understand us and relate to us—even more than any woman on earth!

Man's best support is a very dear friend. —Cicero

:)

We can cry with our sisters and girlfriends, but we can also cry to God. Our friends aren't always available; but God, our perfect friend, is. Notice the emotion David shared with God in Psalm 142:1–5:

> I cry aloud to the LORD;
>> I lift up my voice to the LORD for mercy.
> I pour out my complaint before him;
>> before him I tell my trouble.
>
> When my spirit grows faint within me,
>> it is you who know my way.
> In the path where I walk
>> men have hidden a snare for me.
> Look to my right and see;
>> no one is concerned for me.
> I have no refuge;
>> no one cares for my life.
>
> I cry to you, O LORD;
>> I say, "You are my refuge,
>> my portion in the land of the living."

God's friendship is our portion. It is more complete than any woman-to-woman friendship can be.

What a perfect friend we have in God! When we recognize this—when we understand that he is the one and only Friend who can meet all of our needs—then we don't have to be as clingy or needy toward other people. Jesus declared the two greatest commandments to be "Love the Lord your God with all your heart and with all your soul and with all your mind" and "Love your neighbor as yourself" (Matthew 22:37, 39). They're in that order for a reason. As we learn to love God more fully and completely, loving other people gets a whole lot easier!

That's why, as positive friends, we need to focus on building that relationship with the Perfect Friend first. When we get to know our perfect God, we can accept the fact that people aren't perfect and live with a little more love, grace, and forgiveness toward them. Receiving God's unfailing love into our lives makes us rich with a wealth of joy and peace that only a perfect love can give. We are stronger friends when we are first strong in the Lord.

And that's our charge to you. Becoming a positive friend doesn't start by tediously following all of the principles we have shared with you in this book. It starts by joining in a love relationship with the Perfect Friend, God himself. Through the power of the Holy Spirit at work in your life, you can become the positive friend you have always wanted to be. It's not about your own power. It's about his!

Just in Case You've Never Met Him

If you have never entered into a relationship with Jesus Christ, we want to take this opportunity to introduce you.

Romans 3:22–25 says:

We are made right in God's sight when we trust in Jesus Christ to take away our sins. And we all can be saved in this same way, no matter who we are or what we have done. For all have sinned; all fall short of God's glorious standard. Yet now God in his gracious kindness declares us not guilty. He has done this through Christ Jesus, who has freed us by taking away our sins. For God sent Jesus to take the punishment for our sins and to satisfy God's anger against us. We are made right with God when we believe that Jesus shed his blood, sacrificing his life for us. (NLT)

You see, Jesus came to this earth out of love for you and me. He gave his life willingly, so that our sins can be forgiven. We can have eternal life, because he rose from the dead. How do we start? Believe what he says in Ephesians 2:8–9: "For it is by grace you have been saved, through faith—and this not from yourselves, it is the gift of God-not by words, so that no one can boast."

If you would like to receive his gift of salvation, begin today by acknowledging him as Lord. You can pray something like this: Lord Jesus, I recognize that I am a sinner, and I can't possibly work my way to heaven. Thank you for offering the gift of salvation through your son, Jesus. I believe he died on the cross for my sins and that he rose on the third day. Thank you for forgiving me of my sin. From this day forward I want to begin to follow you and be your friend. In Jesus' name I pray, amen.

If you took a step of faith today, we rejoice! We encourage you to grow together with other friends in the faith by joining a local Bible-believing church or Bible study. Let us know if we can do anything to encourage your walk with him.

POWER POINT

⬤ **Read:** John 3:1–21. How do you enter into a relationship with God? Have you ever taken that step of faith? What are some of the qualities, words, and actions you most appreciate about Jesus in these passages?

♡ **Pray:** Perfect heavenly Father, I adore you! You are the Creator of the stars, the heavens, the mountains, and the oceans, yet you still care about me. I am amazed and humbled that you want to have a relationship with me! What a privilege it is to go to you, knowing that you faithfully love and forgive me. I want to draw closer to you in a deep and abiding relationship. Thank you for being my strength, my portion, and my Perfect Friend. There is no one else who can meet my needs like you! Help me to be a good friend to others and to live out

284

the principles of positive friendship through the power of your Holy Spirit. In Jesus' name I pray, amen.

💡 **Remember:** "Know that the LORD is God. It is he who made us, and we are his; we are his people, the sheep of his pasture" (Psalm 100:3).

☺ **Do:** Set aside time today to be alone with God. In that special time, worship him. Draw close to him in a loving relationship. Look to him as your closest friend. Allow him to meet your needs and give you a sense of purpose and peace. (If you don't already do so, plan to meet with God like this on a daily basis. Spending regular time in prayer and in the study of God's Word is positively life changing!)

Over the next few days, thumb through the chapters in this book and highlight the passages that are particularly meaningful to you. Go over the memory verses from each Power Point and remind yourself of God's great power and love toward you.

Notes

Introduction: Treasures from Heaven

1. John Cook, ed., *The Book of Positive Quotations* (Minneapolis: Fairview Press, 1993), 90.

Chapter 1: A True Friend

1. Dr. Deborah Newman, *A Woman's Search for Worth* (Wheaton, Ill.: Tyndale House Publishers, 2002), 22.

Chapter 2: The Spice of Life

1. Tim LaHaye, The Spirit-Controlled Temperament (Wheaton, Ill.: Tyndale House Publishers, 1973), 23.

2. Cook, *Positive Quotations,* 107.

3. Louise Bachelder, ed., *A Selection on Friendship* (White Plains, N.Y.: Peter Pauper Press, 1966), 26.

4. Roy B. Zuck, ed., *The Speaker's Quote Book* (Grand Rapids: Kregel Publications, 1997), 159.

Chapter 4: Woman to Woman

1. E-mail dated August 8, 2002. Author unknown.

Chapter 5: Cheerleaders

1. Cheri Fuller, *The Fragrance of Kindness* (Nashville: J. Countryman, 2000), 114.

2. Cook, *Positive Quotations,* 91.

3. Used by permission of Jeannie Patterson of Colleyville, Texas.

Chapter 7: Generating Generosity

1. Gary Chapman, *The Five Love Languages* (Chicago: Northfield Publishing, 1992), 73–75.

Chapter 11: Cycles of Friendships

1. Ben Johnson as quoted in Bachelder, ed., *Selection on Friendship,* 8.

Chapter 12: Faith-Filled Friends

1. Zuck, *Speaker's Quote Book,* 152.

2. Anne Peters, "Sisters in Christ." Used by permission of Anne Peters, Plano, Texas, 2002.

Chapter 13: Living It Out

1. E-mail dated June 27, 2003. Author unknown.

2. B. B. McKinney, "Let Others See Jesus in You." Copyright 1924, renewed 1952. *Baptist Hymnal* (Nashville: Convention Press, 1975), 294.

Chapter 14: Confronting with Love

1. Webster's College Dictionary—ed., s.v. "humility."

2. Walter B. Knight, ed., *Knight's Master Book of New Illustrations* (Grand Rapids: Eerdmans Publishing, 1956), 38.

3. Dale Carnegie, *How to Win Friends and Influence People,* revised edition, (New York: Pocket Books, 1981), 210.

4. Ibid, 207–208.

Chapter 16: Mind Games

    1. Zuck, *Speaker's Quote Book,* 155.

Chapter 17: Grace Received, Grace Given

    1. Zuck, *Speaker's Quote Book,* 155.

    2. Ibid.

Never Underestimate the Power of a Positive Woman!

The Power of a Positive Mom
ISBN 1-58229-163-2

The Power of a Positive Mom (Gift Edition)
ISBN 1-58229-291-4

This best-selling series by Karol Ladd offers you five ways to be a positive influence in the lives of those you love. One of the most amazing things about these books—the comment heard over and over—is that they share practical suggestions that are really doable!

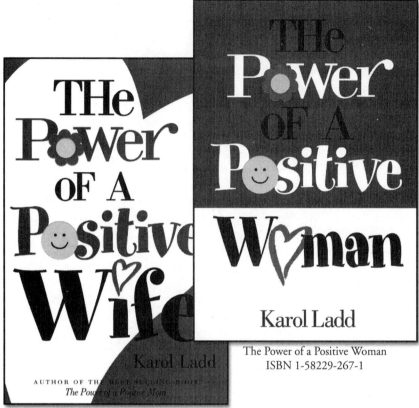

The Power of a Positive Woman
ISBN 1-58229-267-1

The Power of a Positive Wife
ISBN 1-58229-306-6

Each of these books offers seven power-filled principles that will change the way you interact with others forever. In addition to these solid principles, each chapter includes four "Power Points":

- a *scripture* for you to read
- a *prayer* for power in your relationship
- a *verse* for you to memorize
- an *action step* to help you put your positive influence into action

Once you've read one, you'll want to read them all. You, too, can join the thousands of women who are becoming positive, powerful influences in the lives of their family and friends.

James Riny Bros   243 A
    Ⓡ a the light - Bennet Creek
    Ⓡ Route 10